Through
It All, I'm Still Blessed

WOMEN'S COMPILATION PROJECT

Volume 3

Featuring:

Tamara Auguste
Regina Hall-Barbour
Asiah Farrar
Alisha Glover
Taril Gravely
Phyllis Hill
Jocelyn House
Barbara B. Killingsworth
LaTonya McKellery
L'Tarra Moore
Velma Ramos
Loretta Scott
Normia Vázquez Scales
Lajuana Weathers
Fay Wright

Published by
Again I Rise Publishing
Chicago, Illinois

Printed in the United States of America

ISBN: 978-0-9986148-2-3

Library of Congress Control Number: 2017909523

Cover and Interior Design by Jessica Tilles/TWA Solutions

All stories appear courtesy of the authors, unless otherwise noted.

Scriptures used are taken from the New King James Version Bible.

The Women's Compilation Project is hosted by Mutual Partners Association, which is nonprofit organization that implement after-school and summer programs for youth in urban communities. The proceeds from this book will help pay for youth to attend after-school and summer programs that teach character development, self-esteem, leadership skills and experiential learning through fun activities such as theater, music, art, dance and sports.

Acknowledgments

First and foremost, I would like to thank my Lord and Savior Jesus Christ for entrusting me with this project. Truly, without Him, none of this would have been possible. I would like to thank my mother, Mary Loretta Burns, for her love and support. You are an amazing woman who taught me to be a giver and to be loving and compassionate toward others. Mom, you have been my lifetime support system and I appreciate the love you show me daily. I love you with all my heart! I am very grateful to my husband, Abdoulaye Diarrassouba's, for his support, love, and daily encouragement. God truly blessed me the day we met. I would like to thank my late father, Leroy Tripplett, who always believed in me. Whenever I thought I could not do something, he would say, "Baby, you can do it." He was such a wonderful dad who taught me the philosophy of life and how to live life intentionally. I would like to thank my extended family as well for always supporting me in the many endeavors I have embarked upon; Lord knows I have done a few.

God has placed some of the most amazing people in my life. I would specifically like to thank all the women who have consistently supported The Experience Now® and The Girlfriend's Weekend Retreats. These women have been amazing and I truly consider all of them the sisters I never had. With deep gratitude, I would like to thank all the women who participated in The Women's Compilation Project. I do not take your participation lightly. You opened your hearts to this project and entrusted me throughout the process of creating this book. I know it's God's will and His divine order that we all have come together to contribute to something greater than ourselves. I am forever thankful for your obedience to God's call to participate in this project. I could not have done this without your loyalty and commitment.

In addition, I would like to thank my trusted mentor, Deborah Dillon, who inspired me many years ago to start my own business and in 2006, I made that dream a reality and started a nonprofit organization. I could not have done that without her guidance and motivation. Throughout the years, she has given me encouragement; I am thankful to have Deb in my life. Thank you, Julie Tofilon, for editing this project.

Thank you all from the bottom of my heart.

Bridget Burns-Diarrassoba
Publisher

Table of Contents

≫ TAMARA AGUSTE ≪

My True One and Only

My True One and Only

Does anyone have a Bible? I need a Bible! At 30 years of age, an urgency to obtain one and dive into its pages was pressing. I wasn't sure why, yet at that moment, all those who I had turned to hadn't been able to provide the direction, assurance, and comfort I needed from the last 48 hours!

An aunt had left one behind... Thank you so much! God show me what you want me to see... The book of Isaiah... In the next couple of days, I bit and chewed, researched and reviewed. What does this have to do with my situation, which was growing more surreal daily and by the minute? How do I apply the lesson of the Bible to me, God? I turned to my outlet since 14 years old, my journal... Vomiting out my experience, the chaotic whirlwind that gives voice to another had manifested. Ok, God! I'm here... It's been a long while since I picked up a Bible. I remember I used to write out the words of my Children's Bible just for fun... Was that the last time I actually read one? Maybe it hadn't been since my First Communion when I received a pocket Bible. I remember looking through it; it was so pretty and ornate. At 7, I was more disappointed that I hadn't been transformed after receiving God's host than concerned about reading the small print.

In between then and my Bible quest, I sought You, God-for over two decades. I dove into nature theology of Native Americans in high school; in college, I sat in silent meditation at Lutheran chapel in the midst of candles; my friends and I visited a Baptist church and had my first ever peach cobbler at the Pastor's home. I was terrified visiting another church, which must have been demonic in nature. During University, I visited a mosque and my good friend later gave me a Quran. I studied with a Sikh and even communed with Hari Krishnas. I shared my learning of his Hindu faith with my good friend, as my International Studies minor opened the exploration of World Religion and Multicultural Art. I joined Campus Ministry and fellowshipped; I attended chapel and went on retreats with others. Upon graduation, I headed to Central America, ushering into two years of my deferred calling of teaching! From what I was told, I was now the first visibly recognized woman of African descent to join that international corps.

By age 24, it was confirmed that the holy order vows I knew to be my life's calling as a nun were dissolved to only that of my missionary vows of community building, spirituality, living simply and social justice. I knew God was leading me out of MY will! After allowing me to witness first-hand, during my missionary assignment, the practices of Americans and in-house rectory lifestyles, God was sanctifying my mind. Also, my earlier three-year high school employment as a convent evening-shift, switchboard operator revealed that the sake of religious appearance was not GOD'S WILL for me.

I returned to the States with full-time employment as an Assistant Director to an all-girls group. I had volunteered for years with my employer in high school and was an actual founding member of the group and its business venture. The

Executive Director/female Pastor had been my mentor for years in shaping me into a speaker and front-product of the not-for-profit organization. She was like a second mom who I had confided in and sought emotional console and support, especially during my teenage years. She had aided me in finding my voice and esteem, when my upbringing was a culture of upholding the family name - being seen and not heard. Through it all, God kept my gullible, first-generation American mind, as other ventures were enticed, but God always has a way of escape, even in my naiveté.

The details from then to 30-something years of age are in my yet-to-be-released best-seller, God willing!!! In my whirlwind, Maman Fifine (my maternal grandmother, Josephine,) spoke wisdom to me. She said that it didn't matter what I had learned. The fact is that there is Only One True Living God that I was raised knowing. She called me back to faith.

My cousin then invited me to church. I was glad to have some direction. The Woodlawn neighborhood became my home away from home. I applied to volunteer with Children's Church, and periodically would sit in and assist as I was needed. On one particular Wednesday Bible Study, I set aside my conviction that once one is baptized in a faith, one is always baptized in that faith. I resolved to make an adult public declaration to myself, by myself, and for myself before Abba Father that I was now under the control of the Holy Spirit and desired with all my being to accept JESUS CHRIST as My Personal Lord and Saviour! A personal vow was made to My Lord that never again would another being or that created be prioritized before My Sovereign God and Lord of my Life - CHRIST JESUS!!! HAVE YOUR WAY HOLY SPIRIT!!!!

As God continued to prove Himself faithful at every turn, lick, and kick this world presents, I sought Him more, hungering for His Will. I knew that I was the apple of My Daddy's eye; He entrusted me to such treacherous trials and tribulations, while protectively hedging me

in His loving arms! My thoughts and atmosphere were continually filled with God's Word and praise was all I had to offer!!! I saw God's favor in ALL areas of my life and I was so humbled and grateful. I know the experience of a lift of standard and the humbling of a Holy Spirit heavyweight knockout blow! Daughter, it doesn't take all that for Me to hear you ... I AM with you! I even hear your silent whimpers! GLORY!!!!

As a babe in Christ, in my early thirties, the doors were flying open in the midst of a tsunami. I subleased a north-side unit on Chicago's lakefront and was invited by my building security to come visit her church on the northwest side. The two Wednesday Bible studies I attended were a shedding of the dams of my soul! JESUS! Release and deliverance became true to my existence. FORGIVENESS IS REAL!!! I now knew an active surrender to Christ Jesus, which surpassed my wildest understanding! New employment - where are the paychecks - literally? A house my dad bought for me in Florida or the biggest condo unit in a building across the way from a what would-be non-paying job!?!? How did the unit get paid for a year and a half? Whole Food shopping and eating – I didn't know about government support then--- Piggy bank bus fare and 2 mite tithes... MY GOD SHOWED UP AND OUT IN EVERY INSTANCE! Thank you dad and Daddy! You are MY LIVING, RIGHT NOW GOD!!!

Beloved, Ask for Knowledge, Wisdom and Understanding. You know your light can shine so bright in the midst of darkness that without accountability you'll wake to a bushel smothering the last trace element of Oxygen keeping you alive. Ungodly options do present themselves as you cleave to and are elevated in the

Lord. My sister and mom started to go to a new church plant at the exact same time I started attending church on the northwest side. After two weeks, they were done! No way! GOD IS SO GOOD! Taste and see... You have to keep going, I said. I'll even come with you for moral support! I walked in and didn't sit down... It was testimony time and I knew I had a right-now testimony and praise! Crucify the judgment calls T. After a couple of visits, my Spirit woman said, Nice presentation, but this church isn't for you! Never will you be my shepherd is what I said from the onset. Well, I allowed myself to get STUCK there anyway until God literally shut sin down six years later! The Blood of Jesus covers all... I am eternally grateful Lord GOD!

At 40, I finally got spun awoke out of the numbness of being led astray down "my will" continuum which expanded the latter of 16 years! Forgive me Father. Break me Lord! Let the dross be removed! Prune ME Abba!!! Work out the log in my own eye! PURGE ME, Daddy! Thank You for the chastening. I will my will to line up to Your Will! In You, I live! I move! I have my being! ABSOLUTELY! I give thanks to the Lord my God for placing a KNOW in my Spirit Woman! YES to that which is of My ABBA's Will... NO to that which is not of my ABBA's Will! And Amen!!! Giving Thanks to the Power of Prayer, Praise, and Thanksgiving in the name of the Father, Son, and Holy Ghost!

I'm finally back Home at Outreach Community Church of God In Christ, training up a generation in the ways of the Lord!!! My good shepherd leads by THE GOOD SHEPHERD!!! Christ Bride is blessed. Territories are being expanded for God's Kingdom and Glory! We are becoming more like Christ- doers of good and righteousness. We are eagles soaring and finding personal eternal rest in Jesus Christ!

We serve a True, One and Only Living I Am, who is worth being prioritized as the Absolute choice to His Will. Watch and pray, while staying on your post of praise! WHEN you slip or fall, repent, turn away and press on actively towards the Highest Calling- Jesus the Lord of Lords and King of Kings. Remember to forgive and share Jesus' agape, especially with those who deliver purposed betrayal-sealed kisses.

Ask God to personally KNOW Him and the door is opened. **Seek** those, all nations, who need to know LOVE. **Knock** on the hearts of others with your "right now" testimony!!!

Our children's, children's, children depend on your purpose and call. One Body! One Spirit! One Accord!!! Resting in Christ Jesus! Rehoboth! Alleluiah!

Tamara Auguste is a first-generation Haitian-American who Lives to Love and Loves to Live. She is an independent contractual worker with a calling to teach all ages and discipling youth. Tamara and her tribe of estrogen, daughters Allende, Merci, and Noah Selah, are growing in God's divine purpose and might. She is an Ambassador for Christ Jesus, in whom she finds her roar and rest. Thank you mom, Marie Michele… L'union Fait La Force de Famille Auguste! To God Be All the Glory! It is so….

≫ REGINA HALL-BARBOUR ≪

Spiritual Love Affair

Spiritual Love Affair

It is Monday evening and Sister Sophisticated was on her way home from a restaurant, which was her daily routine after her eight hours at work. She could barely wait to get home and get out of her tight girdle, which was killing her. She also badly wanted to take off those tight fitting navy blue stilettos she had to squeeze into, which perfectly matched the outfit she just had to wear today for a special business luncheon.

As she stepped into her apartment, she headed right to her soft, perfumed-smelling peach, genuine leather couch that she just managed to purchase after saving up for some time. This is about the only thing she does have in her apartment, besides her bed, due to her love for clothes, which she frequently purchased with her small limited income.

As she laid there, her mind immediately went back to the life-changing word she'd heard last evening at the mental health conference, which takes place yearly in New Jersey. Dr. Lisa Frank was the keynote speaker for this year, along with Dr. Mary Ann Echols, and Evangelist Cheryl Foster. Not only was Sister Sophisticated impressed by the strength Dr. Frank projected in her teaching, but her articulation and anointing were equally as impressive. Dr. Frank was not the only person that impressed her that evening; Brother Cute pie did so as well. After greeting him yesterday evening at church and seeing his sincere expressions of worship last evening at the services, she knew she had to have this man.

As she laid there scheming on how she was going to get this man, she managed to doze off and fall asleep. While she was sleeping, she began to dream.

While working on her computer at work, the phone rang. It was her girlfriend, Sister Desperate. She asked Sister Sophisticated if she wanted to go to a prayer breakfast for entrepreneurs with her because she heard there were going to be eligible, single men. Sister Sophisticated had only gone to work on this Saturday to print a report for her boss. She left work, went home and found her Versace suit, which was balled up in the corner of her room. She shook the wrinkles out, showered, dressed and ran out of the house. On reaching the Hilton Hotel, where the prayer breakfast was being held, she found they had already begun. The worship was so powerful that the prophetic word began to come forth. When the minister came to her, she began to prophesy to her that she was going to get married. Sister Sophisticated fell out in the spirit. When she came to herself, the breakfast was over. She got herself together and found Sister Desperate and they began to talk. She noticed that there were only women there, except for one man who was old enough to be her father. He was bald and was wearing an orange tweed suit, and he had the nerve to look at her and grin. She turned her head, picked up her black Coach purse and left with Sister Desperate. When they arrived to the car, she got the surprise of her life. Brother Cute pie was standing there waiting for her.

The phone ringing awakened her and scared her half to death. It was her girlfriend, Sister Desperate. "Girl, I'm going to kill you. The phone scared me half to death! You interrupted my dream! Brother Cute pie was waiting for me at my car," Sister Sophisticated said, becoming fully awake.

They both laughed. "Well, I am calling to tell you that I found a ski resort where a lot of single men hang out, so give up a trip to the hair salon and nails this month and Macy's department store and you'll have enough to go.

"Girl, I'm going back to sleep!" They hung up. To her amazement, she fell right back asleep and went right back into the dream....

Brother Cute pie sat in the car with her and said, "I was in prayer today and the Lord revealed to me that you were to be my wife. I know we haven't known each other a long time and that I've only been saved for a few weeks, but when it's God's will, all of that doesn't matter." She screamed and said, "Yes, I will marry you."

The dream shifted and she found herself at the altar with Brother Cute pie. She heard the words, "You may now kiss your bride."

The dream shifted again and they rode up in front of the hotel lobby in the Bahamas in a horse carriage. Brother Cute pie lifted her up and carried her to their suite. They entered their room and he sat her on the couch and began to stare into her eyes while holding her tight. He got up, opened their bedroom sliding glass doors to hear and view their ocean scenery while she went to take her shower. The wind from the ocean was trying to blow the candles out but they would not go out. The door opened and Sister Sophisticated stepped out from the bathroom wearing her honeymoon attire. When she peeked into the room, she saw him sitting at the table listening to the music and she squealed with delight. He just looked up and smiled. She walked slowly over to him and sat beside him and they began to feed their dinner to each other. As he fed her, she ran her nails (that she and her maid of honor glued on while sitting in the limo waiting for the wedding procession to start) through his soft, jet black hair. While she fed him, he ran his fingers through her hair (getting stuck occasionally due to the fake hair her stylist glued in the day before the wedding). He started to whisper in her ear while she sat there giggling like a high school teenager. She grabbed his hands and pulled him outside onto the balcony and they stood their holding each other, watching the ocean and gazing at the full moon, which was extremely large and red that night. Since he stood over 6 feet tall, and she stood only 5feet 2 inches, he laid her head on his chest and said, "Listen to my heartbeat. It is saying I love you." And she blushed.

The doorbell rang and Sister Sophisticated woke up. She ran to the door with panic in her eyes, only to find the landlord coming to collect her rent. By coming to her, he feels like she would pay him on time but she never does. She went to her bedroom and pushed all the clothes off her bed to get the money from under her mattress. She went back to the door and gave him the money. "You are $100 short."

"You will get the rest on Friday," she responded with a smile on her face. He just shook his head as he began to leave and said, "Here's your mail."

She closed the door and threw the mail on the kitchen counter. She knew it was all bills; mainly credit card bills from every dress store that offers credit cards. She lay back down on the couch. "He had to wake me up. I was just about to... Something told her to pick up the mail, and when she did, she saw a letter from her girlfriend, who lives in Atlanta by the name of Evangelist Joy. She pepped up and opened the letter while walking to the refrigerator to get a soda, which was the only thing in there since she does not cook. She began to read the letter.

Praise God, girlfriend,

"Is all well? I was in prayer this week for you and I picked up your depression and frustration about not having a mate. As I prayed for

you, the Lord interrupted me and told me to get a pen and paper to write to you, and this is what He is saying to you.

"*Everyone longs to give themselves completely to someone, to have a deep soulful relationship with another, to be loved thoroughly, and exclusively. But God says to a Christian, "No, not until you are satisfied, fulfilled, and content with being loved by Me and Me alone…*

"*Then, will you be capable of the perfect human relationship that I have planned for you.*

You will never be united with another until you are united with Me—exclusive of anyone or anything else, exclusive of any other desires or longings.

"*I want you to stop planning, stop wishing, and allow me to give you the most thrilling plan ever —one that you cannot imagine. I want you to have the best. Please, allow me to bring it to you. You just keep watching Me, expecting the greatest things—keep experiencing the satisfaction that I am. Keep listening and learning the things I tell you. You just wait. That's all. Do not be anxious. Do not worry. Do not look around at the things others have gotten or that I have given them. Do not look at the things you think you want. You just keep looking up to me, or you will Miss what I want to show you.*

"*Then, when you are ready, I will surprise you with a love far more wonderful than any you would dream of. You see, until you are ready and until the one I have for you is ready, (I am working even at this moment to have both of you ready at the same time), until you are both satisfied exclusively with Me, you will never know fulfillment, for mine is the perfect love. And dear one, I want you to have this most wonderful love. I want you to see a picture of your relationship with me, and to enjoy maturely and concretely the everlasting union of beauty, perfection, and love that I offer you with Myself. Know that I love you utterly. I AM GOD.*"

Well, girlfriend, I trust you will receive this awesome invitation that God has taken time to extend to you. I will be in touch shortly. Take care.

Love, Evangelist Joy

After Sister Sophisticated read the letter, she immediately began to weep in the presence of the Lord. She began to praise God for all He had done in taking out this time to get her attention. She had watched so many of her girlfriends get married and felt then like she would never be chosen. When God had finished talking to her, she fell into a deep sleep in His presence. After being asleep for only a few minutes, the phone rang. It was Brother Cute pie.

Regina Hall-Barbour is an international minister, speaker, author, and counselor. She is a native of Newark, New Jersey where she attended Arts High School. Regina received her Bachelor's degree from Rutgers University in Psychology and her Master's degree from Liberty University in Marriage and Family Therapy. She also attended two outstanding universities in her course of study: Lincoln University and Howard University. Regina has worked in the social services field for over thirty years, where she worked as a substance abuse counselor, family counselor, pastoral counselor, and mental health clinician. She had the privilege of sitting under the tutelage of the great late Bishop Norman Wagner of Youngstown, Ohio where she served as an associate minister. Regina had the opportunity to minister in England, Germany, Italy, Canada, and throughout the states for conferences, retreats, and other events. She is passionate about hosting prophetic and marriage retreats. Regina is the author of the book: Saved, Single, and Seeking to Be Satisfied, which sold over 10,000 copies just by word of mouth. She currently resides in Lynchburg, Virginia and believes that ministry begins at home, as she ministers to her husband, Brent and her son, Micaiah. For speaking engagements, Regina can be reached at reginaabarbour@gmail.com

❊ ASIAH FARRAR ❊

Greater is She Who is Within Me

Greater is She Who is Within Me

B lack women are beyond dope! Plain and simple. The black woman is the mother of civilization. She is a divine creature.

"So what the heck is wrong with me then?! Nikki?! Hello?! If we were placed on this earth to be fruitful and multiply, what the heck is my job if I can't? What's my purpose?" Nichol jumped out of her slump on the couch after receiving a text message from an old classmate. She'd once again been invited to *someone else's* baby shower. She didn't understand why God had not blessed her with a child and she was already pushing 60 years old! 32 to be exact, but you get my drift. "Nichol, at this point, unless you're trying to get knocked up by Remy, Tito, or Mr. Dom Perignon, you need to find yourself a husband before you think about having a child, honey," Nikki advised. Nichol responded sarcastically with rolling eyes, as she made herself a cocktail, "I thought I had one. We *all* thought I had one. The seamstress that was altering my wedding dress thought I had one. Everyone who received a "Save the Date" invitation thought I had one. But anyway! If I must wait on someone that deserves to be with me to have a child, I might as well hang it up."

Before Nikki could begin encouraging Nichol, as she always did, she was interrupted by the loud sound of Nichol's techno ringtone coming out of her new Samsung Galaxy. "He may not come when you want Him but He's ALWAYS on time! Thank you, God, for saving me from the Queen of the Party Poopers. Now who the heck is this? I've lost all my contacts and now I can't screen my calls." Nichol answered the phone and was greeted by a guy she had been dealing with for about two months. His contract was almost over and he'd soon be replaced by a new man of the hour, or week. Apathetically, with a little sarcasm of course, Nichol answered, "well hello Lawrence, how are you?" "I'm aight. I was thinking about you and decided to reach out." What Lawrence really meant was, he was scrolling down his timeline and noticed a cute new picture Nichol posted so he decided to call. Nichol responded, "new day, same ol' game," and continued listening to the bull that was coming through her Bluetooth until she finally decided to end the madness. "I'm about to hop in the shower. I'll call you a little later." Lawrence, being Lawrence, responded with the norm. "Can I join you?" Nichol hung up in his face and returned to her date with Mr. Tito.

"9 o'clock on a Saturday evening, in the middle of the summer, and I'm sitting in the house alone. I want company, but I don't feel like being bothered. *Ugh*! I might as well get me a couple of cats and start knitting." "Well, Nichol, you always have me." "Nikki, you don't count! Go away. As much as you're around we might as well be together and live happily ever after." "*Hmm*, that would be weird, girlfriend." Nichol didn't understand what was going on with her love life. It was a straight up joke! After separating from the man she thought was her soulmate, it seemed like the only men left were goal-oriented clowns, attractive dogs (the female version,) cornballs with a great sense of humor, snakes with great careers, and a ton of other great weirdos that she didn't see a future with. She just couldn't figure out what was wrong. She met guys in a bunch of different places, from the hole-in-the-wall bar to professional networking events. No matter where they were from or what they had going on, there were always deal breakers. After venting to Nikki for the next hour or so, Nichol decided to lay down and fall asleep listening to Jill mixed with a little Erykah.

As the praise team sang Nikki's favorite song by Travis Greene, Intentional, she hoped that while she was praise dancing, Nichol was listening to the words and taking heed. Nichol enjoyed Sunday morning worship but, instead of taking the message and applying it accordingly, she applied it to the lives of others, especially those that she felt played her. However, we are only accountable for ourselves and can only work on ourselves. We cannot control other people; we can only control our reactions to them. After service ended, Nichol and Nikki greeted everyone and got started on their weekly Sunday routine.

While waiting in the car outside of The Crab House, Nichol scrolled through her newsfeed as she always did during idle moments. "Nikki it's obvious that I'm cursed. Did you see Amin's post on Facebook? His girlfriend, the one he apparently forgot to tell me about while we were together, is pregnant with his son." With a confused look, Nikki asked "and exactly what does that have to do with you? Why do you believe you're cursed? Girl, you better thank God you didn't have that woman's stepchild. Ha!" "Why are you confused? You haven't noticed that almost every person that I have dealt with after 'him whose name I shall not mention' was blessed with a child, in one instance children, either while or right after we were together? God is doing me dirty for real!"

Nikki shook her head and decided not to comment. Their crabs were finished steaming and being seasoned well. Nichol paid for them and drove home. There was nothing like jumbo blue claw crabs, males of course, and the finest wine on a Sunday afternoon in Nichol's backyard on her plush patio couches. After changing their clothes and tying their hair back in a ponytail, Nichol and Nikki sat on the patio and went to work with some 90s R&B jamming in the background.

"What's up? Can you clean me out one? I'll keep you company." Nichol's neighbor, Ryan, who happened to be the finest man in America, yelled out across the fence from his patio next door. He had the most inviting smile with those deep dimples and pearly whites. He was in the middle of grilling himself a rib eye and decided to take a shot at spending some quality time with Ms. Nichol. Smiling from ear to ear with BOTH dimples on display, Nichol squinted her eyes and yelled out in the most anxious, nonchalant voice, "hey Ryan! I'm taking it in shortly. Maybe next time." Nichol lied through her teeth as her mouth turned Ryan down once again and her heart, mind, and Nikki all sulked in disappointment. "While you're over here trying to figure out what's going on with Tom, Dick, and Harry, Ryan has been checking for you and you continue to avoid him." Nichol rolled her eyes and went back to her crabs. Nikki just couldn't understand what the problem was. "He's checking for a whole lot of broads obviously. There's a different chick running in and out of that house every weekend. I'm telling you girl; God's been playing me." Nichol chuckled but truly believed what she was saying.

"Nichol, let me ask you a question. Why haven't you given your old car to Ashley yet?" "Because she STILL has not restored her license. She has unpaid parking tickets in almost every county in New Jersey. On top of that, I'm sure she will have every guy she deals with behind the wheel and their papers probably aren't straight either. She's not responsible. Shall I continue?" "But Nichol, she just had that baby and was hired at Nordstrom last week. She needs a car." Nichol responded as she shook her head and spit out crab shells, "that's not my problem boo. I had that car forever and she's not about to tear it up as soon as she gets it. But wait, what does this have to do with the price of gas going up?! I'm trying to vent and you're talking about Ashley." Nikki smiled and explained, "Nichol, you haven't given Ashley that car because you don't believe she's responsible enough to receive it and take care of it. You think as soon as she gets it, it'll be taken away from her anyway so why even bother. She needs to get it together first, right?" Nichol started clapping and yelled "Bingo! Now back to *my* life."

Nikki continued. "Are you prepared to be someone's *good thing*? Have you healed from your last relationship or are you looking for another man to fix what was damaged? What type of man are you looking for anyway? Do you want to be a single mother? Are you prepared to have a healthy baby? What you put in your body has a major impact in fertility. Are you preparing your body to carry and nurture a baby? Shall I continue?" Nichol rolled her eyes and continued eating as if she wasn't listening but, she actually felt like a light bulb had turned on in her head.

"All I'm saying is, God knows the desires of your heart and he hears your prayers but, MY God is not in the business of blessing a mess. You need to establish order in your life and prepare yourself for what you're asking for. Get in your Word, be obedient, and remember that God's answers are always either "Yes," "Not yet," or "No, I have something else in mind."

Nikki was interrupted by the doorbell. "Who is it!?" Nichol yelled from the back patio. She was too lazy to walk through the house to the front door. She heard a male voice but couldn't make out the name. She decided to walk around to the front of the house and saw a familiar face. With a smile on his face and sparkling brown eyes, the mystery man asked, "Are you alone?" Nichol hesitated before responding. "Yes. Why?" He quickly responded, "Nik I miss you. Can we talk?"

In the movies, there is sometimes a good angel and a bad angel on opposite shoulders representing conflicting views on a subject. In the real world, sometimes the good angel is within us, while the bad angel is what's displayed to society; hence, Nikki versus Nichol. As Nichol stood frozen as if time had stopped, she could hear her mother's voice saying, "if you always do what you've always done, you'll always get what you've always gotten." Even with that in mind, at this point, she didn't allow that wisdom embedded within, or the voice of her inner self, Nikki, deter her from what SHE believed was the best thing for her.

Nichol finally responded as she walked to the backyard. "Sure. We can talk. Come to the back. Do you want me to clean you out a crab?"

Known for her passion, diligence, and humble spirit, Asiah Farrar is a young woman from Irvington, NJ with a mission to excel and defy the stereotypes placed on her. She has earned a Bachelor's Degree in Business Management from Rutgers University, School of Business, and currently works in the Marketing division of a

Fortune 500 company. Asiah is the Co-Founder and Coach of Jersey Diamond All-Stars, an all-star cheerleading team based out of her hometown. Passionate about community engagement and women's empowerment, Asiah has made it her obligation to mentor the youth and young women in the city, ensuring they have an outlet and the resources required to have a rewarding future. In addition, Asiah is an active member of the Secret Place of Praise, Inc. Church, in Plainfield, NJ, where she leads the usher ministry. Though Asiah seems to have a plate full with mentoring, work, coaching, and church involvement, she still makes time to spend with family and friends. This is Asiah's first piece of literature, an introduction to a series of upcoming novels. Be on the lookout for this amazing young woman!

≫ ALISHA GLOVER ≪

From Past to Purpose

From Past to Purpose

As a young person, it never dawned on me the importance of my destiny, or the importance of my struggles, traumas, mishaps, and victories in my overall purpose. I never even imagined my life as a story, let alone one that would be printed and shared with others around the world. Everyone has a story, everyone has a past, and everyone has a purpose. It's easy to accept that we all have a story and a past, but do we really believe that we have purpose? Ask yourself: do you believe that the events that have occurred in your life (good or bad, accidental or intentional, self-inflicted or not) all serve an overall purpose?

Like millions of other people, my life wasn't one of perfection or ease. On the other hand, it wasn't so terrible either. I come from a military family, and had a pretty decent upbringing. But like many other families, we had our fair share of dysfunction. Throughout my childhood, I was never one who really fit in, although I had my circle of friends. They were great friends, who remain today, but I never felt like I was part of the "in" crowd. I also never thought I was a pretty girl, just an oddball who was smart and kind of talented. I carried a hefty amount of low self-esteem for my entire childhood, and a good part of my young adult life. But because I was a "master of masking",

31

no one really knew this. I was an overachiever-- everything I did, I did well. I was addicted to the approval of others. I never wanted to face perceived "failure" in any area of my life. I was a straight-A student, talented singer and musician, great at making friends, and great at entertaining people of all ages. I always "had it together." If I ever "missed the mark", gave the wrong answer, or didn't succeed at something really simple, I would beat myself up over the "failure."

I remember participating in the district spelling bee in the sixth grade. I misspelled the word "cabin" with two b's. Oh, that was THE WORST! I tried to hold onto my pride for as long as I could, but I didn't even make it back to my seat in the audience before I burst into tears. How could I fail at such an easy word? And to top it off, how dare I lose it in front of others! That was when I added yet another "layer" to my personality...."never let 'em see you sweat." Showing emotions signifies weakness.

Then there was my being introduced to molestation.... several offenders. Who knew what that was, at the age of 5, 6, and even 12? How did we deal with that in the 70s and 80s? Well, I said nothing....just brushed it under the carpet and kept moving forward. Especially when I was made to believe it was a "secret" between me and the babysitter, or even emotionally manipulated by others. In fact, they even made me believe that I actively participated in allowing another person to invade my personal space and body, and that if they were found out, I would also be guilty because I participated. That would be "failure" to me, so I kept it a secret.

I didn't realize what was going on between my parents until around junior high school when they first separated. There were things that I saw and witnessed from that time through high school that changed my perception of my parents, even into adulthood. I remember being a "daddy's girl" when I was younger, but then all of that changed in junior high and high school. With the change of having to be raised in a single parent household, and being told to stop running to the counselor's office (because it was nobody's business what was going on at home), I became angry and began plotting my escape from home. I began seeking attention, so much that I ended up being elected class clown of my high school graduating class. I even tried to run away from home, but that lasted about 2 hours. It was just too cold out there, living in a fort surrounded by dirt, grubs, and worms... *sigh*...

Nonetheless, I earned a scholarship to college and moved almost 3000 miles away to DC to attend Howard University. FREE AT LAST, or so I thought. During my 1st semester, I went buck wild-- party, party, party! Even to the point to where I made a 1.8 GPA! What in the world? Failing classes, staying home from class watching talk shows, etc. But I knew I couldn't fail OUT of school—that would mean having to return home. Wasn't having that! So, I made it through 4 years of undergrad, finished with a 2.95 GPA, and then things began to get really real. Looking back, I really believe that I tried to self-validate my worth by "flexing the power of my femininity" as a young adult. I mean, that was the one thing I had control of...or did I? Well, up to this point I was having a good time. I'd had many life-changing experiences, some good and some bad. But the most memorable came at the age of 25-- I got pregnant.

Who was ready to be a mother? Not me. I always said I never knew what I would do if I got pregnant—I'd cross that bridge if I ever got there. Well the time came for me to make a decision. What would my mom think? What would my friends and family think? So, I decided to have an abortion. UUUGH, it killed me to do that. How could I? I was a bad person! And of all days, it happened the Saturday before Mother's Day. I knew my parents would be disappointed in me, but what about God? Well, in my mind He was already disappointed in me. How much worse could it get? And BOY was it a let-down to my parents! How could I make SUCH A MISTAKE? How embarrassing was this? That's when I realized that I'd been living my life for others who never gave me any permission to make mistakes. I'd lived my life as this perceived "perfect" child-- well guess what, I'M NOT PERFECT! But deep down, I still thought I had to be, and I was driving myself crazy trying to be.

As I moved on in my 20s, I still found myself needing validation, the feeling of significance, and acceptance. I didn't realize then, that I WAS significant. I'd been very instrumental in various movements and projects. I had great leadership capabilities, I was creative, but I just couldn't see it. I didn't accept MYSELF. I didn't love and appreciate my own gifts. I focused on what others had, or what I THOUGHT they had, not even realizing that many of the people in my circle were dealing with the same "stuff." I wanted to "fit in" like I thought many of my friends did, but in reality I was different. Then along came a man who saw that. He was 9 years older than me, and saw the maturity and value in me that I couldn't see. He accepted many of the scars I'd accumulated up until then. He was responsible and mature, almost too good to be true. I thought I'd mess this up. I mean, why would someone who had his stuff together, seemed grounded and financially secure, want to be with me? But I figured, oh well, let me try it-- let's see if I'm REAL relationship material. And lo and behold, it worked!... for about 3 years. What we later learned (and admitted to each other) was that we BOTH had levels of immaturity that played a role in the failure of the relationship. But I also discovered there is such a thing as a good man who would accept me for me, and that I actually had the capability to love, respect, and fully commit to a man who made me feel safe.

As I moved on to try and heal from that relationship, I purchased a home, and continued to work toward establishing myself financially. I began taking a more serious interest in my music, yet I was still searching for significance. Even more, I began to search for more of God. I was getting older now, and knew that it was past time to get my life in order on the spiritual side. I hadn't had a church home that I felt comfortable with since I moved to DC, and I was also looking to share my life with someone; as I was in my early 30s and still hadn't found anyone who I felt I could fully trust.

I eventually met my husband. I felt that he was gentle, understanding, and accepting. He made me feel free enough to be transparent about where I'd been in life. He made me feel safe. He was also a man of God. I figured, "He would be the one to cover me, and help me to move closer to God." Upon noticing some behaviors and thought patterns indicative of my childhood dysfunction, he suggested that I get help from a counselor. I thought, "You know what? That's a great idea."

You see, although I had areas of low self-esteem and fear among other things, I was resilient. I was a fighter. Remember, I don't like to fail, right? So I was determined to get better. During my counseling sessions, I'd dealt with buried hurt and pain from childhood and even uncovered buried events of molestation. I sought healing and closure to marred and blemished relationships with my parents. I'd begun to build confidence in who God had created me to be. I'd begun to learn more about and apply the Word of God to my life, along with the teachings I was receiving in our church.

Simultaneously, I endured several forms of abuse from my husband during the course of my marriage: emotional, mental, and physical. It was an unhealthy situation for me. But as his wife, I still chose to try to keep issues under our roof. I tried to capitalize on the good moments we had, and that's what I chose to share on the outside. But in reality, I'd become isolated from my friends and family. I no longer had a social life.

What I later came to realize was that I'd connected with a controlling man who also suffered from a dysfunctional upbringing, coupled with deep rooted rejection, pain and low self-esteem issues. They'd just manifested differently. I'd eventually stopped going to counseling because I was convinced I was getting better in the areas of my past. Plus, I didn't want to arrive to sessions upset, having to explain why I was hurting. I thought I could keep this foolishness a secret.

As my relationship with God strengthened, accountability set in and I'd finally had enough of being mistreated. And those were the words I used-- "Yeah….I won't be enduring this type of treatment anymore…*Sir!*" And when I made that decision, ALL HELL BROKE LOOSE. I faced slander, rumors, and more emotional abuse.

Although I couldn't understand why this was happening, I did understand that the REAL ENEMY was trying to assassinate my character, and tear me down in ways that would've ordinarily caused me to shrink back. But I'd grown so much in God and had so much appreciation for who He'd made me to be, that fleeing from this fight was not an option. The only thing I could do was to "…stand, and see the salvation of the Lord…"(Ex 14:13). See, my marriage was aired-out in front of the entire congregation, where we both served in leadership. So I had to be mindful of my conduct, my speech, my attitude, and my responses. I knew people were looking for a reaction to my situation. I had to live my life in a way to prove the lies to be just that…lies. Eventually, my husband left the church.

We ended up divorced, but not without our fair share of drama. I was left with questions, a broken heart and a mound of debt (I owned everything). I cried; I got angry. I went through two bankruptcies, five foreclosures, & faced many stress-related illnesses. And I didn't even know a credit score could drop to the 400s! The restoration process took all of six years. I never quit; I never died. I returned to, and completed, counseling. Thanks to God, I was able to see the same therapist. I got certified as both a Professional Coach as well as a Christian Life Coach. I returned to my music, and opened a business aside from my regular nine-to-five. At the time of this writing, I've recorded and released a single, and am completing my first solo album.

What did I learn?
- I never needed ANYONE to help me get closer to God;
- I've grown to love & respect who God created me to be;
- I learned to celebrate myself, and celebrate my individuality;
- Feeling and expressing emotions is healthy;
- Making mistakes is OK. It's how I learn;
- No one's perfect; And finally,
- To never compromise who I am for any one person or situation.

My experiences and victories led me to develop a passion for empowering those who struggle with fear, low self-esteem, and corrupt thinking, which prevent them from living life in confidence and abundance: MY PAST SHAPED MY PURPOSE.

My experiences and victories led me to develop a passion for empowering those who struggle with fear, low self-esteem, and corrupt thinking, which prevent them from living life in confidence and abundance: MY PAST SHAPED MY PURPOSE.

We ALL have a story, we ALL have a past. We experience things in life, not only to gain victory, but to serve as examples to others who encounter the same. "Your life is necessary for someone else's recovery" (*Bishop Melvin E Blake, Jr., In His Image Christian Ministries*). Although many of us have been through the fire, we don't have to look burnt, nor smell like smoke! That makes us more than conquerors! So…what is your purpose?

Story title provided by: Pastor Cheryl D. Blake, In His Image Christian Ministries

Coined as a Divine Muse by some, Seattle native Alisha Glover has always been inspired by the fine arts; namely music.

Aside from her passion for music, Alisha has a passion for people. Nurturing her ability to inspire and lead, Alisha entered the world of coaching in 2010 with a certification as a Professional Coach, and moved on as a certified Christian Life Coach in 2015. As a coach, her main areas of focus are conflict management, interpersonal relationships, and leadership development. She uses her music as a vehicle to reach people; to touch, inspire, and empower all within earshot.

Alisha is purpose-driven, and believes that every person should maximize the potential of every known area of his/her gifting for the purpose of reaching, uplifting and encouraging others. "For only what you do for Christ will last…"

≫ TARIL GRAVELY ≪

Angel of Mine

Angel of Mine

When I was fourteen months old, I lost my mother while she was giving birth to twins. My father married a wonderful, loving and caring woman to help raise his eleven children. She treated us as her very own children. My father and stepmother later had seven children. We had some really good times together as a family. My sisters and I would make a playhouse out of planks. We would take a round stick of wood, a butcher knife and trim all of the bark off of it until it became pretty and yellow to make dolls. We would take some cloth and make a bonnet, blouse, skirt, and dress. We would also play hopscotch and jump rope. My brothers and I would play bingo, checkers, dominoes, and horseshoes. We would sit around, take two spoons, turn them backward, beat them together against our hands to make music and sing.

We grew up together as blood sisters and brothers with much love and was taught to share, help one another and work the farm so we would know how to survive. We were never hungry or cold because Mama and Papa would deny themselves to make sure we had what was needed. They always raised a garden to make sure we had plenty to eat.

After losing my mother, I became attached to one of my sisters because of her loving, caring and humble spirit. She was a compassionate person who could comfort me in a time of need. I could always talk to her about anything because she had a listening ear and an understanding heart. Although I do not remember my mother, at the age of sixteen, God sent her to me in a vision. She told me to come and go with her and sit right down at the feet of Jesus. After this experience, the Lord blessed my soul to sing, shout and praise him. I was able to thank him for his goodness, mercy, and kindness.

I had a vision where God showed me a star, which came down and turned into an ink pen and wrote my name in Zion. He told me to go and I will go with you, open up your mouth and I will speak for you. He also told me that I can't walk like I used to walk, talk like I used to talk. He told me that I have to love everybody no matter how they walk or how they talk. He put a needle in my side and it turned into a door key. He told me I have a bad heart, so he took out the stony heart and gave me a heart of flesh.

Then he told me that he holds the big key and little key to unlock the kingdom to let me in. He said that I have got to die and can't live, and his power killed me and made me alive, which meant that I became born again. He took me to the school of grace and told me he was the teacher. He told me he was going to give me the recognition of service and a promotion too. He gave me the report card and I made the highest grade in the classroom. Finally, he told me that when I graduate from this world he holds my diploma.

I joined the church the fourth Saturday in October 1964. I was blessed to be baptized the fourth Sunday in November 1964. I met my husband at the church in 1965 and got married the following year on March 12, 1966. I remember our first date being enjoyable because we had a nice conversation while going to visit his sister and parents before he took me back home. A week later, we went out to eat and a friend approached me and he got upset. He became jealous and began to raise his voice and pitched a fit while accusing me of being with the man. I felt sad, hurt and disgusted because he embarrassed me in public. I had never been so humiliated and disrespected in my life. Although I recognized his disturbing and unpredictable behavior while dating him, I thought he would change and become a better person.

After dating for six months, he gave me an engagement ring. I accepted the ring and we got married six months later at his parents' home in Virginia. I moved from North Carolina to Virginia where he lived with his parents. Approximately, two months later, my wedding band got lost. After frequently reminding him, he finally replaced the entire set within the same year. His father was a kind, loving and understanding person, but his mother was an unrighteous person. I felt safe and secure when his father was home because he would tell my husband to treat me with respect. Conversely, I felt fearful and humiliated in the presence of his mother because of her rude and disrespectful behavior. I could tell she never liked me based on her facial expression when having a conversation.

When my father-in-law in April 1966, I felt very sad, heartbroken and lonesome because he was always by my side whenever I needed him. We lived with my husband's parents for six years before moving into our own home in 1972. This was when my life became a disaster on Horror Hill.

I was not excited about moving into my home because the Lord had shown me that my mother-in-law had moved in without permission. This meant that she was going to take control of my household. As time went on, his mother was able to manipulate and persuade him to mistreat, demean, and undermine me. His erratic behavior revealed a deceitful, envious, malicious and violent man. I was frightened and feared for my life the entire time living in my home. My husband was never satisfied no matter how hard I tried. Nothing was good enough for him. I would cook breakfast every morning, pack our lunch, and clean the house before going to work every day. After constantly being on my feet working hard on the job, I would come home and can different types of fruits and vegetables from our garden during the summer and winter.

While trying to fall asleep, my husband would go to the bathroom and call my name like he was in a barrel, which scared me. He would also beat on the wall in another room to make it seem as if someone was outside the home. I immediately realized that he was trying to make me lose my mind. He would slide his hand down the wall when he was walking down the hallway. He tried to kill me three times. The first time, he had a round stick of wood and told me that he would beat my brains out of my head. The second time, he tried to choke me to death and God stepped in and pleaded my case. God took his hands out from around my neck and put them straight up in the air out of harm's way. The third time, he put a pillow over my face and held it for twenty minutes, but God intervened and he left the room.

In 1994, on a warm and sunny morning, my husband told me we were going riding. I thought we were going uptown to do some shopping, but I noticed we were going in the opposite direction. We drove approximately forty minutes until we arrived at a mental institution. I was afraid to ask the reason for bringing me, so I got out of the car and went with him inside the building. While we were waiting, my husband told me that a mental health counselor he had seen a week ago told him to have me admitted. He left me standing at the front desk while he signed paperwork to have me admitted. The clinical supervisor took me to a room and told me that my husband had paid a man that worked there to keep me in the institution. She told me that based on her observation and my state of mind there was nothing wrong with me. Also, she mentioned that the nurses were going to make me take medication against my will. She said that I should, however, not swallow it because I do not need it. She told me to hold on and wait because she was working on getting me released.

During my stay at the institution, people were kicking down doors, tearing doors off hinges and fighting, which was very disturbing. I would stay awake all night long because my nerves were on edge not knowing what was going to happen at any given time. It seemed as if I was tied to a chain and unable to move. I was living a nightmare, which was hard to believe in this troubling situation that left me feeling terrified for my life

My brother, sisters, and friend came to visit and provided moral support during my stay at the institution. My friend talked to the clinical supervisor about me having the ability to communicate effectively with others using a sound mind, and the capacity to function in society. She asked the clinical supervisor to release me in her care. She would be responsible for taking care of me and making sure my needs were met. After being institutionalized for three months, I was released in my friend's custody.

It was a new beginning in my life the moment I arrived at my friend's home. She made me feel welcome and safe. I was able to relax and rest in her peaceful home. Her home was a safe haven, which allowed me to heal the wounds of my broken heart and feel love. The sun began to shine again because of the happiness I felt deep in my soul. My life was sweet and so complete because of the love expressed and understanding shown during my pain and suffering. I stayed with my friend for five years until her death in 1999. She was diagnosed with multiple sclerosis and her health began to decline within a year. I became her caregiver until her death. I truly believe that God brought us together to help each other in a time of need.

Although my heart was filled with pain for the loss of my friend, I was blessed to be reunited with my sisters and brothers. They were excited to have me home with them again, which brought back precious memories. I was overjoyed to be in their presence because we were able to sit around and talk about the good times we had growing up on the farm. We were able to attend different functions together, such as yard sales, family reunions, and church. It was a glorious time because my life had come full circle until the loss of my brothers occurred about three years apart. I was sad and hurt because they were no longer here for me to embrace and tell them how much they were loved. Then, approximately six years later, the loss of my sisters occurred less than a year apart, which was devastating. The deaths of my sisters brought about a great change causing my life to never be the same. I felt so empty and lonesome that my heart ached with pain. While I loved both sisters, the sister that understood me like no other family member was no longer able to come to my defense. After the death of my sisters, within a year another sister became confined to the bed due to health problems. Since my sister is only able to feed herself, she is required to have 24-hour care. I assist the aids with providing her medication, bathing her, combing her hair and cooking to make sure her needs were met. I oftentimes feel overwhelmed and exhausted with the number of responsibilities required of me to contribute to her well-being. Nevertheless, I constantly pray to God, asking him to renew my strength and help me to continue taking care of my sister.

Angel of Mine

This angel of mine sent from above has enabled me to survive the raging storm. God has given me the ability to rise above my troubles because he is everywhere present and nowhere absent. He has always been by my side to hide and shield me from danger. God has allowed me to overcome any obstacles because he is the author of peace and not confusion.

 Taril Gravely is a native of Martinsville, VA. She is a graduate of North Carolina Agricultural and Technical State University. She is a humanitarian, activist, educator and poet who enjoys writing short stories, event planning, traveling and spending time with family. Her talents as an avid reader, care giver, facilitator, mentor, music connoisseur aspire her to become an author, motivational speaker and documentarian. Taril is the creator of TMG Enterprises whose founding principle is based on "the desire to inspire people to create passion with purpose."

❧ PHYLLIS HILL ❧

Keep My Night Light On

Keep My Night Light On

I was afraid of the dark as a little girl. Even as an adult, I still do not like a pitch-black house. So, I have nightlights throughout my house, and no one is permitted to touch them because of how I have strategically placed them throughout my home. I know where each one is supposed to be, and I get very upset when they are not in their proper places. I simply do not like to be in dark rooms; I need just a sliver of light. Even when I stay in a hotel, I need a sliver of light. I've even thought about traveling with a nightlight in my suitcase, but then my family would really think I was crazy. But I was afraid of the dark for a long time. You see, long ago, a bad person made me afraid of dark places when they turned my safe place into a place of fear, hurt, pain, regret, doubt, and anger. But, the Light became my way out. Light gave me comfort, brought me peace, and gave me strength.

Growing up, I always felt safe with my grandpa until a bad person invaded our space. I loved my grandpa to the moon and back. I didn't know where my father was, and my mother was not active in my life. Because of this, my grandpa and I had an amazing bond; he even would let me paint his fingernails and put barrettes in his hair! My grandpa was like my dad, and in the mornings, we would sit at the kitchen table drink coffee, eat toast, and talk all day. I always slept with my grandpa, but a bad person also had a bed in that same room. One night, that bad person also decided to sleep with my grandpa. I didn't think anything of it because grandpa had a big bed, and I always slept up under him. That night however, the bad person asked me to play a game with him. He told me I had to be very quiet and that I "couldn't tell nobody." He said that if I told my grandma and grandpa, I would be in a lot of trouble, and I didn't want my grandparents to be mad at me. I trusted this person, and I thought the game would be fun because when you hear the word, "game," you automatically think you are going to have fun. But, it wasn't fun like making snow angels in the snow, playing with my friends or, playing with my dolls. I didn't like this game. The bad person lied; this game was not fun.

I wanted the game to stop, but I didn't know how to make it stop because the bad person told me that grandma and grandpa were going to be mad at me. What could I tell them, when I didn't even understand what was going on? My grandparents slept in separate rooms because they were old and sick. We only watched "He-Haw," "Tony Orlando and Dawn," "The Sonny and Cher Show," "Johnny Cash," and old Westerns. My grandma watched soap operas like, "As the World Turns," but I was not allowed to watch those shows. We did not listen to the radio, and the only records we played were country songs. My grandma once told me ladies who wore short skirts where hookers - the problem was that I didn't know what a hooker was, but I believed my grandma because that's how a child's mind thinks. We believe what we are told by people we trust. I played a game with a person I trusted, but I wanted it to stop, and I needed a way out.

One night, I decided to sleep in my grandma's room. Like my grandpa, she also had a smaller bed in her room. I soon realized that her room was much more peaceful, and it was brighter than grandpa's. I remember those green sheer curtains on the windows in her room; I had a perfect view of the moon and the stars. And, unlike my grandpa who slept like a log, my grandma slept a little lighter, so when the bad person tried to wake me up, he would also wake up my grandma. There were other times when I would hear the bad person call me, and try to lure me back to grandpa's room, but when I heard him, I pretended like I was asleep. I would open my eyes just enough to see his face, and I ignored him. I felt free from the bad person, and, looking back, the Light made me feel stronger.

As time went by and I grew up, I realized what the bad person had done to me... and it made me angry. I was crushed and disgusted with him and with myself. Then, my grandpa died and my grandma's health got worse. Once that happened, my grandma sent me to live with a man I didn't know - their son, my father. She soon died as well and my world crumbled. I was never going home because they were my home, and I began to think that I was to blame. I blamed myself because I thought my actions caused their death. And I had two men in my life: one I didn't know but should have, and the other who was the source of my pain. But, I wasn't a little girl anymore and wasn't I defenseless. I was angry. I no longer had my grandparents, but I had the moonlight. The moonlight became a source of comfort for me because it reminded me of my grandma. I could always see in the dark, so I always made sure I had sheer curtains like grandma. I also had a lock on my door and kept a screw driver under my pillow, but in the process of protecting myself, I became trapped within myself.

Somewhere along the line, I trapped myself in an endless cycle of being wounded and being a warrior; if I wasn't wearing my pain, I was fighting the pain within. I wounded myself for a long time and was mad at everyone in the world, including myself and God. There were times that I would cry myself to sleep and dream about being at home with my grandparents, only to wake up on a wet pillow. I thought that if I had been a good little girl, maybe God would have kept my grandparents alive. I remember watching "The Wiz" and asking the Lord, "If I clicked my heels three times, would He take me back home.?" I thought that if I had been smarter, I would have known what was happening to me and would have stopped it, and if I was brave, I would have told somebody. I thought I was a cursed and wicked little girl that did not deserve happiness. I wanted to go back home, so I promised God that I would be better little girl. But God began to talk to the wounded little girl, and He said that I wasn't going back home.

God revealed to me that I had to leave my source of comfort to reach my destiny. Then, He gave me the opportunity to go back home. I did not recognize the place; nothing was the same, My grandparents' house was gone… blocks of houses were gone, most of the homes had been reduced to patches of grass, and drugs had taken over. I thanked God that my grandparents were not alive. God knew that I would not have survived in that area if my grandparents were alive. I thanked God because he got me out. He had a bigger plan for my life.

Later, God told me to forgive the bad person, and when I began to look back over both our lives, I wondered who had showed the bad person how to do bad things. He didn't always live with us. Maybe something happened to him which cause him to do those bad things to me? I wondered if someone stole his innocence. As I looked back, I knew of one potential predator in our family – my uncle. My uncle made me very uncomfortable. He used to look at me like I was the last chicken wing on earth, and when he looked at me, it would paralyze me in fear. His hugs were scary, and I stayed away from him as much as possible, so I always wondered if he was the source of this problem. God then gave me the task to forgive him, but not to forget what he had done. So, I learned to forgive him and I did not hold the past against him. I could no longer keep him chained to my pain, however, I did not forget what he had done and I never left innocent souls in his care.

Then, God told me to forgive myself. You might think, "Why do I have to forgive myself? I didn't do anything wrong." But I needed to free myself from my own cycle of pain. I had so many should have's, could have's and would have's running through my mind. As children, we sometimes see ourselves as the cause of all problems in our lives. I called myself stupid for not sleeping in the room with my grandma sooner, and I thought myself, "How could I have allowed this to happen? I should have known." But it wasn't my fault, and God did not take my grandparents away from me because I was bad. They were both old and sick, and God sent me away to protect me. God saw my future while I still was stuck in the past.

Finally, I learned that God doesn't take you through a valley so that you can keep your healing to yourself. God revealed to me that my pain was commonplace in both men and women, and that most people don't recognize a person that's in pain. They look at us, but never see the pain in us. So, for those of us who walk in pain, we often feel like outcasts and we don't quite fit in anywhere. We are sometimes angry and misunderstood, and sometimes we are drug addicts, cutters, suicidal, and societies degenerates. We are sometimes bullied, and sometimes, we are the bullies. Some church people calls us sinners, claiming that we have a demonic spirit, but if people would take the time to talk to us, and not at us or judge us, they would find that we are in a lot of pain and realize that we don't know how to deal with it. Booker T. Washington was once quoted as saying, "There are two ways of exerting one's strength: one is pushing down, the other is pulling up."

God did not heal me just for myself. God healed me to help someone else; to be for them what I wished someone would had been for me. To listen to them, and not to tell them the cliché, "if I can do it then they can do it too." To walk with them, and help them on their own personal healing journey, to give them a hug, and let them have a good cry. Perhaps they will allow me to share my battle scares and my journey. I want them to know that I am here for them, and know that I won't judge their actions because I have asked God to never let me forget my own. And, one day, I pray that they will ask me how I made it through. I will explain to them about the Light, and how it was God's Light at the end of my tunnel. I will explain how the enemy thought I would destroyed but that God had another plan. I will tell them that God can heal their pain, if they let him. And if you allow Him, you will also understand that pain can have a purpose and help someone too. I have many nightlights throughout my house, but God's Light shines brightest and keeps me safe in dark times. Every night, I love looking at the moon and the stars, and I know God keeps the night light on just for me.

 I am a wife, mother, grandmother, daughter, sister, friend, mentor, teacher, author and a speaker. I am a Certified Christian Life Coach, a graduate of New Life Coaching Inc and I love of the Lord. As women, we wear many hats and sometimes those hats create issues in our lives. Those hats can make our lives messy, stressful, difficult and leave us wounded.

But I know God has a balm for every wound and His word can bring peace to any situation. Christian Coaching can bring a fresh perspective and new insight to an issue. God created us to overcome life's issues and not succumb to them. And it is my desire is to help women live their best lives now, regardless of the hat they wearing.

≫ JOCELYN HOUSE ≪

Your Works Are Wonderful

Your Works Are Wonderful

During my generation, fitting in was something important for young girls growing up, and being popular was a major thing. I grew up during a time when fair skin was *beautiful and thin was the sexy thing for young girls to earn big brownie points with teenage boys.* Personally, I had coco-marshmallow skin and willow-thick hair that a comb would never dare to manage to get through without breaking. My face was round, and in those days, I would have been known as a "thick" girl and more of a friend to the guys than someone they would want to date. This was actually a blessing in disguise to me, because I was a sister to most, managed to have a lot of guy friends, and became well-known to both guys and girls.

I focused more on my academics while also participating in many academic and social organizations in school rather than socializing in groups or hanging out. I started attending school in a Suburban Community through a program called, "The Metropolitan Council for Education Opportunity" or, "The Metco Program," which transports inner-city children from imbalanced schools to the suburbs. I really struggled throughout the middle of my developmental stages… because I tried to be someone I wasn't. By this, I mean I tried to fit in with the other kids my age, but often they treated me like I didn't exist. Home life for me was stable and well grounded. I grew up with a good spiritual foundation as a child; I attended church every Sunday. The rule in my house was, if you don't go to church, don't dare ask to go anywhere the next weekend. And although my mother would make us go, she only went on special occasions. Sometimes I felt like I was living in two worlds -- one with peace of mind, and another with a lot of chaos. At home we were free to explore spirituality. It was a safe place to discuss church and prayer. At school and around my friends I kept my spirituality hidden. I felt that if I showed that side of me I would be laughed at or judged, so I kept spirituality to myself so that I would fit in. I was young and already spiritually grounded. When most just wanted to play, I just wanted to pray. I remember one instance that happened when my so-called "friends" wanted me to fight someone in elementary school and I went home that afternoon, dropped on my knees, and prayed about it. I felt so awful. I asked God to please forgive me and to let her forgive me one day in her heart. I hoped that she understood that I just wanted friends.

I was taught to pray and I did. I prayed through every situation in my life, whether good or bad. I started saying my prayers when I was young, and when I visited my grandparents, my cousin taught me "The Lord's Prayer." We always had to pray before we went to bed at night – well, I felt we prayed for everything growing up in those days. It was like day and night coming from the north to the south, and the level of respect expected from us was totally different, even to this day. For example, we weren't allowed to call adults by their first name and certain words weren't considered appropriate. I started from that day forward saying my prayers morning, noon, and night - I prayed through all situations and every circumstance, and would get frustrated at times because things didn't happen as quick as I wanted them to happen, even though I know prayer doesn't work that way. God doesn't work that way. I've learned prayer is about establishing a personal relationship with God. When you're building a personal connection with God, praying from your heart establishes that relationship.

I also learned there was no special ways to pray. I spoke to God out loud in a quiet place and learned that you didn't have to have any special prayer to talk to Him, and I learned that *"if I ask, I shall receive* "(Mathew 7:7). Understanding the power of prayer and knowing that prayer can give you a deeper connection with God became truth to me. During High School, I was going through a lot of different family crises and circumstances. I felt like my life was falling apart. I was struggling with transitioning into a young lady living on my own already at the age of 16 due to conflicting personalities between mom and me. Times was difficult for me learning to be independent and taking care of myself without the assistance of others. Although I was young and on my own, I felt confident God was stabilizing my foundation and would restore the walls that were tumbling down before me.

I was becoming more comfortable with my spirituality and no longer hiding it as much. I knew how to pray and had an understanding that building one's faith required focusing on the Word of God. I would stay in the word and fall out. I don't know what to call it, but during this time I had a strange feeling that my life was being prepared for something big. I just couldn't pinpoint what it was. Later in my early twenties, I found out what that feeling was. I was about to enter into a major battle zone. I had always had faith and confidence in

God, but this new war zone seemed like I couldn't win alone. After accomplishing great things in my early twenties, I had a good Job and was a mother of a great son. My son was my greatest accomplishment. He was my life source and gave me hope to continue to live and not just exist. Growing up, my son was such a great kid; I knew God was looking out for me. I believe that there is a saying, "God looks out for the elders, babies, fools, and the sick," or something of that nature. When my son was 4 months old, I believe that's when the battle started. I started experiencing a lot of issues with my body; I was sick throughout most of his childhood, going back and forth to see doctors, but he never complained or gave me any problems. He's always been a great child and student. I always told people that I thought he felt bad for me, but now I know that I'm truly blessed. I remember asking God to cover me when I found out I was pregnant like any other mother, and I pray for my son daily more than I pray for myself. I asked God to lead and guide me with my parenting because I knew nothing about being a parent. I taught him the best I could, and what I knew, which was prayer and his spiritual principles.

I was sick for most of his upbringing and my prayer had always been to let me live long enough to raise him to know God and take care of himself in this world. I raised him to trust in the Lord, and to let Him lead and guide him through all his situations and circumstances.

Thinking back when I was younger, I do not recall having any health issues. And from what I remember, I was a healthy and active teenager who lived a fairly decent lifestyle. I remember personal issues I had then more than anything, for instance, things I did that I felt ashamed of or was embarrassed by. I would pray and ask for forgiveness constantly, and then struggle with the same thing again and again, falling into that same cycle over and over.

My life would always become chaotic when I found myself outside of my safety zone, which was being in alignment with God and his word. I loved the lord and knew my place was with him and not with worldly thing, but often I found myself going back and forth. I lived outside my spiritual realm throughout my early twenties, but I continued going to church some Sundays and prayed daily. After years of hard work, education, and remaining focused, having learned from my mistakes in life and having an increased prayer life, I still found myself in darkness, my physical infirmities had increased. I felt like a brick building with a solid foundation that was being knocked down level by level. My life was becoming a pillow of unexplained body aches and pains. I couldn't understand why my life's journey appeared to be coming to an end when I was only at the beginning. Sure, I made mistakes like anyone else, but I stayed devoted to God. Could my life be ending before it even begun?

As the illness progressed, I felt like a prisoner, trapped in a sick body. I soon became house-bound because my health issues took over my body completely. I went from doctor to doctor, had multiple surgeries, and was in and out of hospitals. I even had to go through more medical challenges throughout the last two decades, and now I live with an ileostomy pouch and I self-catheterize. After being misdiagnosed several times, after my last surgery, the doctors finally made the right diagnoses…Lupus. Most of the treatment and surgeries were unnecessary if I was properly diagnosed correctly. After much pondering over my life and all I went through, I have to believe I went through my circumstances in life for a reason, as I have always looked at situations as life lessons. I look back at what happened and see it was preparing me for my future. I now understand that God already knows a situation in my life before I did. You see, I knew of God and I had a praying spirit throughout my life. I really thought I had a great connection with God by utilizing him like most of us do - when things got hard, what do you do? You pray right? I went to church, but only when it was convenient or for traditional holidays.

Then came the battle; the fight of my life. It was like a rollercoaster. I couldn't understand why I kept losing and being defeated. I was praying and nothing was happening. I felt like God wasn't there…like I was in this battle alone. Then realization set in. I realized I had to surrender completely. I couldn't be Luke warm. I had to live by the will of God, and I picked up my Bible and started reading the word of God to know Him for myself. God is not a God for Convenience. He wants us to know him wholeheartedly. There is a difference between going to church, knowing of God, and knowing God for yourself. I believe God has led and guided me down this road to lead me back to Him. I've faced a lot of adversities in my life, which I did not allow to hinder me. Rather, I have taken them as blessings that God has placed before me to strengthen me. I know my foundation was always there and I have always known how to utilize it, especially in the face of defeat. I always knew how to prepare for battle, but through learning and reading the word of God I've found that you should always be ready to stand strong with the Lord.

Once my spiritual principles increased, everything started coming together for good. circumstances as well. I knew that "*I could do all things through Christ who strengthens me*" (Philippians 4:13). I didn't just want to go from the bed to the couch, and I refused to let the bed take my strength. I got up every day and made sure my son had a hot meal and a clean house to come home to. No matter how much pain, or how many difficulties I was going through, I knew from my experience and professional knowledge that my influence played a big role in my child's emotional development. My prayer to God was to let me live long enough to guide my son to Him. I pleaded to God to lead my son and guide him throughout his life in all circumstances, to strengthen him to be a man of faith and godly ambition in this world, and to make him the man who will be part of the world's solutions and not part of the world's problems.

God is truly amazing and answers our prayers. I know this because we have been through many storms and have managed to get through the rain. We see the rainbow and slowly recognize the colors day by day. I thank God for my walk daily and all the trials and tribulations that happened in my life. I truly believe that everything in my life happened to lead me to my purpose and to give me a better understanding of how to live by God's will. I learned to depend on God and not on people, places and things. Most importantly, I had to surrender and learn to "*Trust in the Lord, with all my heart and lean not on my own understanding*" (Proverb 3:5). I learned to get up daily and wake up with the Word of God, to set my day, for when I set my atmosphere and lived by God's will, this helped me lead my child according to the Lord's principles. The Bible says, "*Train up a child in a way he should go: and when he is old, he will not depart from it.*" I'm truly blessed to say now that he does pray on his own daily and has learned to read the Word of God. This is important because he is now a young adult and can still get preyed upon by evil, or step outside the spiritual realm. However, I believe that with a strong spiritual foundation, he will always defeat all odds when he has God.

We go through circumstances in life to increase our faith and to bring us closer to or back to God. I'm staying dedicated to him because He gave me a second chance at life and to live right this time. God stayed with me through sickness and health and through good and bad times. He truly loves and cherishes me when no one else will, and has always been there when my son and I needed him the most. Today, I still have health challenges but I am doing better. Knowing that my strength is not in self but in God, I can endure this race with peace.

"*The Lord himself goes before you and will be with you; he will never leave you nor forsake you. Do not be afraid; do not be discouraged*" (Deuteronomy 31:8).

THANK YOU FOR YOUR WORKS… I'M WONDERFULLY MADE.

My name is Jocelyn House. I currently live in Scituate, Ma. I was born in Sumter S.C, but raised in Boston, Ma. I was inspired to share my story after facing many medical challenges for the past two decades. I am the founder of Ostomies Awareness, which is a non-profit organization that was created to bring support and awareness for those who live with ostomies. I'm also a Christian and Secular life coach, with a niche of psychotherapy for addiction and psych. My Passion is to continue to help others regain comfort and confidence back in their everyday life. www.ostomieswareness.com

≫ BARBARA B. KILLINGSWORTH ≪

Because He Cares

Because He Cares

1 Peter 5:7

O h, what hard lessons I had to learn about the cares of this world and the care of God for me. We really do go through more than we should ever have to. I am sure that at one time or another the struggle is known to all of us. When we come into the knowledge of His greatness, we start to mend from whatever pain has been inflicted, either by ourselves or by others. We know that all our pains do not come from the enemy, but we allow certain things to take place as a result of our decisions.

Often times we think that we can change someone, but little do we know that can't happen unless they want to change. God cares about our tears and fears. He cares that we are set up for failure by our surroundings. That is why we should never give up on our dreams. We need to *look to the hills from whence cometh our help because our help comes from the Lord who made Heaven and earth.* (Psalm 121). I found myself trying to make him see that I did love him, but he was not interested in my love; having control was most important to him. If I said I loved him, his response was, "I know you do". If I said that I didn't love him, his response was, "You do love me and I will make you love me." He didn't treat me right because he didn't know how.

There were instances of abuse that I can tell you about, such as the time I just got a new job and on the way to work I was taken to an area across the Burlington Bristol Bridge under the pretense of a marriage that had already gone bad. No one could imagine the amount of trauma my body, soul and mind endured that day. He parked the car, locked the doors and immediately straddled me. I began to cry because at that moment I knew I was going to die. He needed me to believe that I was not supposed to gain control of my own life. I was choked, smothered, repeatedly smacked, and mentally beat down. I pleaded and promised him that I wouldn't tell anyone and to just let me go. He opened the door and pushed me out. After I fell out of the car, he dragged me across the stones and my pelvic area was in so much pain that I began to bleed out. I thank God that He cared for me and didn't allow the enemy to kill me that day.

My family lived on both sides of our home and could hear me scream both day and night from years of constant abuse. Even after a restraining order, I'd still have to call the police because he would come through the cellar and break the door just to get in. I have to admit there were times I'd allow him back in through the sickness of trying to prove my love for him once again. I truly wanted to get away from him because he was so cruel. Simple choices like what underwear to put on or what clothes I wanted to wear was never my own decision.

Domestic violence is something that is most understood with someone who has experienced the pain of not acknowledging their own self-worth. Many say that abuse is a cycle. It typically happens because of how one was raised in a home of violence and from what I have experienced, this was sometimes true. My son abused women that he dated, his father abused me and his grandfather abused his wife.

My prayer is that any woman who reads this should know that she is not alone. This is my testimony and if God had not cared about me I would have not lived through the beatings, hits, humiliation and the constant overwhelming suicidal ideations. At that time, I believe I tried to take my life at least seven times. God has allowed me to move forward and to forgive. It was very difficult to completely let go and let God fix the sadness within, from all the abuse. Because He cares, I was truly able to cast all the cares of my past. The moment you realize that the Lord is with you, you will not have to worry anymore. You must get to the point where you know who you are in Christ. God wants us to speak things that be not as though they were. For many years, I never thought that I would get out of that bondage. The enemy was sent to destroy me and he didn't care who he had to use to do it. Everything is a choice and I chose LIFE. God loves me and He cares for me.

There is a song that I always wanted to sing. The song is called "Your Tears" by Bishop Paul Morton. For years, just hearing the song would make me cry and I knew that if I attempted to sing it, no one would be able understand one word because of the place those powerful words took me. You see, that is what pain will do to you. But guess what? I sing it all the time now in my heart because God has truly wiped my tears away. I don't have to cry anymore because of the abuse. Yes, it's going to be a glorious time when we get to Heaven and because of His infinite wisdom and His grace we can still smile and rejoice for the promise of God is at hand. We must never give up because God sits high and looks down low with His eternal glory. After you have suffered for a while God will make you perfect, establish you, strengthen you, and settle you. I love the Lord because He first loved me. What a mighty God we serve. He will never leave us or forsake us. Just think, when this is all over we **SHALL** receive a crown of glory. Praise God for different tears of joy.

Apply this to your daily walk....
Matthew 13:22
Mark 4:19

A Letter to the Lord
Psalm 139:14

Dear Lord,

Please grant us the things we need and the desires of our hearts. Lord, I need a home and I need transportation. I need to be closer to you. My desire is not to waver at all. Lord, free me from any wavering spirit. You have been so good to me. My unhappiness is because of my self-sabotage. Lord, help me to find myself. Give me that child-like faith.

I need spiritual strength like never before. As a woman of God, where do I go to deliver your messages? I need to be set free. I am locked up inside. Lord, I need you to set me free. I know that wherever you send me was predestined. I know that it was a part of the plan. The journey has been extremely long, although I know that your time is not my time. Lord, I know that it is all for the making of a true soldier. I know that you will never put more on me than I can bear; therefore, I must trust you. I'm feeling so uneasy. I need to know where to start. Lord, lead me to my purpose in you. Cleanse me and purge me of anything that is not like you. I want to be used by you.

Guide my how, when, where, and why of my very being.

Take away any lonely feeling. Lord, take away negative emotions that may destroy me. Occupy me with a spark of life that will extinguish any feelings of unworthiness.

For I am fearfully and wonderfully made! I come face to face before God to have Spiritual Restoration!

Cordially your child,

The Woman of God you made me

P.S. more than a conqueror (Romans 8:31-39)

Barbara B. Killingsworth moved to Georgia over 30 years ago from New Jersey. She is a wife and a mother of six children. She is a grandmother of seventeen and a great grandmother of two. She is a licensed and Ordained Outreach Pastor. Her credentials are in Early Childhood Development, NACCA National Credential Administration, Quality Assist, Positive Discipline instructor, Parent Educator and facilitator, Georgia State University CDA, Business owner of Lady K Kiddie Kare, CEO of Power of Knowledge Consulting and Training services, and a Mental Health Paraprofessional. She is very passionate about her family and their success. Very grateful to her husband and the support of her family. Her constant prayer is for the covering of her family and friends.

❊ LATONYA LAWSON-MCKELLERY ❊

Finding My Purpose as a Military Wife

Finding My Purpose as a Military Wife

"Ask, and it will be given to you; seek and you will find; knock and the door will be opened to you. For everyone who asks receives; he who seeks finds; and to him who knocks the door will be opened."
- Matthew 7: 7-8

It was 1990, I was 22-years-old and in the middle of my junior year at North Carolina Central University in Durham, North Carolina when I first met my husband. We were at an event at Seymour Johnson Air Force Base in Goldsboro, NC. We talked all night and began seeing each other from that point on. When we began dating, he had already been in the United States Air Force for 3 years; he joined in 1987. We dated for a year, and in that year, it was fun, exciting, and adventurous. We traveled and we had some of the same hobbies, but we came from two different worlds. When we were not together, he was traveling with the military. When I could not go with him, he would come visit me on the weekends and spend time with me at school until he had to be deployed again. It was difficult to manage the relationship, but we continued to make it work. He was deployed for 9 months in 1991 shortly after we began dating - it was not easy because I did not know of his whereabouts for about a month. He would call when he could and sent letters often, and when we did talk, he would tell me all the things that women want to hear like how he was missing home and could not wait to be back with me.

He told me that while he was away, he had begun to reflect on life and how much he wanted us to be closer. He said that he would like to get married when he returned from being deployed… they were the longest 9 months of my life. I was lonely and tried to stay focused on school to keep my mind clear, but he was the love of my life. We wrote each other every week and I would send care packages every chance I got. When he returned, we spent more time together than we used to before he left. We traveled, went on boat rides, worked out together, and began planning our future together. During that time, my mother did not want me in a serious relationship, however I could not help myself for I had fallen for this man. She wanted me to finish school, like any other parent would. My mother would say, "You don't know this man and where he came from," but that didn't stop me from being with him. This man was intelligent, and he had a career with a bright future ahead of him.

Then, I got pregnant with Briana, my first child. We both agreed that we did not want to have a child out of wedlock, so we decided to get married sooner rather than later because he was to be reassigned to another station, and he wanted us there with him. When I informed my mother and father, they were not happy. They didn't want me to keep the child for they felt as though I wasn't ready to be a mother. Instead, I chose a family and to marry the man that could give me that family. My mother came to me and said that the reason she did not want us to get married was because she had heard that he already had a child with a young woman that was close to our family. Well, as always, my mother was right. He did have another child who was 2 years old. I knew nothing about the child nor did he until about 4 months before we were to be married.

In November 1991, we got married and Briana was born in July 1992. Shortly after Briana was born, we moved from North Carolina to the United Kingdom (England). I was 24 years old with my first child and away from family and friends. It was not easy because I wanted to be close to my mother given that I had just given birth to my first child.

Briana was 2 months old when we moved to England. My mother came over for about a month, but thereafter, I had to depend on my husband and extended military family for support. I met great people and God was always there for guidance and the ordering of my footsteps.

I had a hard time in the beginning because I had no family and had to make friends in an environment which I was not familiar with. I had no job, and since I hadn't completed my degree, it was difficult finding a job. So, I enrolled in school, connected with the base chapel, and opened up a home daycare. The amazing thing was that I attended the base chapel after being there for about 3 months; God was always in the midst. I know this because when I walked in, I saw that the pastor was a young man that I had grown up with at my church in NC. We were all raised in the same church and his family was now stationed in United Kingdom. Nothing but God. I connected with him from that point on. But, before that, it was lonely because I had no family and I was always home while Shawn, my husband, was working. He had a career, but I had not completed what I had started, so it took me a while to adjust.

Once I started connecting with people, kick-started my daycare, and began schooling, I finally felt I was going somewhere. The kids enrolled in my daycare were mainly from people who worked with my husband; he was on a crazy work schedule. So, I did daycare around his schedule so that we could spend more time together and travel around Europe. It was a beautiful place to live, and for us to travel was a big thing.

Given that he was always traveling with the Airforce or deployed, I had to meet new people on my own. While we were in the United Kingdom, Shawn was deployed for 3 months in Germany. During this time, we would go back and forth to see each other, and by now, I was used to being there and connected with friends and what I call extended family.

With him gone, running my own business, and going to school, I had to find someone to help me with my baby. Having to find a daycare for her was not easy. So, I found another daycare provider and we took turns watching each other's children while we attend school. Her husband was deployed as well, so she and I began traveling and exploring Europe together.

One of the best things about being a military man's wife was traveling, seeing the world, and meeting new people - people who became friends or extended family. I always knew that God was in the midst of it all. Even today, I still keep in touch with some of the people I connected with and have also established long-lasting relationships with a few of them.

My husband was always working. And when he was not working, he was playing in the Air Force Football League in United Kingdom, so he did not attend church and retreats as much as I did. We were supposed to be in England for four years. However, when the base closed, we were reassigned to San Antonio, TX.

Once again, I had to look for employment, update my resume, get to know the area, find daycare, and meet new people. The one good thing was that the young lady who also did daycare with me in England moved to San Antonio TX as well.

In the middle of the deployment, or moving to our new station, I got sick. After we had been married for four years, I found out that I was eight weeks pregnant with my second child in 1994. After settling in TX, life became hectic. He began work immediately and his career was still successful… I however, had no career and still no degree. I had a 3-year-old child and was pregnant with my second one; and, on top of that, my second child was having kidney problems and would need surgery once she was born. I was lost and scared. What made it worse was that one day when I went to the mailbox, I read a letter that stated that my husband's blood test was complete, and there was 99.99% chance that he was the father of a 5-year-old boy back in North Carolina. My heart dropped. I would like to state this clearly - the child was conceived when we were dating - however, he was not informed until after we had been married for 5 years. Naturally, I was the last to find out; not from him, but from a letter from the child support office. I wanted this to be over so badly.

The question that everyone kept asking was, "Why would you stay with this man?" I love my husband and I did not believe that divorce was the answer. Plus, I felt that I could not take care of my two children alone and I wanted my children to grow up with their father.

I had been taking care of my family and putting my life on hold while he was traveling and working because his career was good. Now, don't get me wrong, my husband was and is a great father. He is smart, intelligent, and knew his job well, but, I guess I was not enough for him.

And when I asked, he stated that he wanted to wait to tell me until after the baby was born given that I was having complications with my pregnancy. Living in San Antonio, TX, I was unable to work at first and unable to go to school. The pay was poor, and on top of that, he now had to pay child support, not just for one child, but for two children.

Again, I began to think about what my mother said 5 years ago, "Wait to get married because you don't really know this man." I thought a year was enough. I was in love and pregnant with his child; he loved me and was so excited about our baby girl. He was even more excited when our second child, Kierra was born in 1995. Our relationship got stronger, but in the back of my mind I didn't think that I could trust him.

He would hang out all night and come home the next day, and sometimes, I would have no clue where he was and would stay up all night.

I had found a local church and an older lady there began to mentor me. She helped me with the girls and I began to look for employment though I was still unable to attend school because of our financial situation at the time.

I applied for a job as a correctional officer and got the job, but I had to wait until I passed the training and 6 weeks of class. I finally got the job, and out of thirty women, only five of us passed. I was excited! For the first time, I was doing something for me and it felt good.

We were there for 3 years until my husband got orders to be relocated and stationed in Hawaii. Yet again, I had to deal with having to look for employment while trying to finish school. Plus, his career was successful.

Hawaii is where I applied for a student hire program and was accepted. At the time, I was 28… almost 29 years old with no degree, no savings, no 401k, and no job. But, I felt this was the time to complete my degree because we were assigned to Hawaii for 4 years while the last 2 assignments were only 2 and 3 years respectively. I enrolled at the Chaminade University of Honolulu, I worked 32 hours a week at the Legal Jag Office for the United States Airforce, and was a full-time student raising a 2-year-old and a 4-year-old. My husband's career was still a success, and by now he had a retirement plan and stable employment. I felt I could not get past that threshold because we were always moving. But now, I had finally found some peace and was putting in a lot of hard work at the same time.

Once again, my husband was deployed for 4 months after we had been there for a year.

I was enrolled in school full time, working 32 hours a week, and had to have someone take care of the girls. Luckily, my parents were always helping us. They paid for Kierra and Briana to go to private school because I was willing to continue on the path that God had opened doors for me to. I had a young lady come in and help with the girls in the evening and on the weekends. The girls were smart and doing well, but were having a hard time adjusting to their father being away. Because of this, I studied when they were asleep because I wanted to give them the attention they needed while they were with me.

Hawaii was beautiful and we began to work on our marriage. After returning from deployment, my husband and I began to do things as a family, and we enjoyed the love of God until I got a call one day from a young lady who said that she had been seeing my husband while he was deployed. I was hurt; it got lonely whenever he was deployed. By this time, I began to pay him with his own coins. My attitude was, "you did it to me, now I will do the same to you."

As a young military wife with two kids, I had to make a lot of sacrifices for the benefit of my family and a lot of my personal goals were put on the back burner. Although I was faced with the obstacles of moving from place to place, being away from family and friends, searching for jobs, trying to finish my degree, and balancing being a mother and wife, I overcame and achieved many of the goals I set for myself. By not allowing things to get in my way or giving excuses, I didn't hold back. I gained great knowledge and experienced many cultures that I otherwise would have never experienced. I want women of all ages to understand that God's timing is everything and that it is never too late to achieve your goals and to not be discouraged when faced with life challenges.

LaTonya Lawson-McKellery, born in Goldsboro NC and is the only Child to Mr. and Mrs. Thomas and Aquanetta Lawson. She enrolled into college at North Carolina Central University, and has completed her undergraduate studies at Chaminade University of Honolulu in Criminal Justice and a minor in Law. She went on to get her Masters in Criminal Justice with a concentration in Psychology and Counseling. She has been married for 26 years with two lovely young ladies, Briana McKellery (25) and Kierra McKellery (22), and is a dedicated leader with 20 years of experience working with military service members, their families, and the private sector in the areas of counseling, mental health/substance abuse, and the criminal justice system.

≫ L'TARRA MOORE ≪

Named for Life

Named for Life

Clay and I have known each other for over 20 years. We met volunteering at an elementary school, and connected over a common interest in helping people. Clay's fraternity organized a group for troubled young boys, and their mission stated that they were determined to change the boys from troubled, to changed and renewed. He would always tell me about the kids he came across, particularly this one young man in the group he met and kept up with. This young man was doing great, he told me. Clay said to me, "I knew he had a rough upbringing and spent some time in a home, but you would not know 'cause he is an excellent young man with great potential and a great sense of humor. One day, while having lunch, I was sharing with Clay how I used to volunteer at a children's home and how much I loved it. I shared with Clay about a little boy named Jax, who grabbed my heart. I noticed Clay looked at me as if he recognized something and was listening intently. I went on to say how I made sure I saw and spent time with him every volunteer opportunity. Clay asked, "Why was the little boy there?" I told him, "Just from observing, I believed he was abused." I also shared with him, "We, the volunteers, were encouraged to love the children in the home more than just knowing their history." Clay asked, "What ended up happening to him?" I explained, "That precious little guy was sent back to his mom, and a few months later, he came back to the home with bruises and broken bones." I remember going to volunteer, and one of the staff members said, "Hi L'Tarra! I have a special assignment for you." I told her, "Oh, ok!" The staff member said, "Come in here and I'll come talk to you." I went into the room and sat down. Then, the staff member came in, sat down across from me and said, "Jax is back." I felt excited because I was going to see him again, then quickly felt sad because I knew what that meant. The staff member went on to say, "Jax is very fragile; he has bruises and some broken bones. I want you to stay here in this room and be with him as long as you can." I could feel tears welling up inside me, but I had to get it together, and quick. The staff member turned back to me and said, "Now, I'm going to give him to you backwards. If he sees you reaching for him, he is going to cry hysterically." So, while I waited, I decided to put some toys out for him and set up a couple of videos. The staff member came in with Jax and handed him to me. With his back against my chest, Jax and I sat peacefully for hours, playing a little and watching videos, all while he whimpered. Clay asked, "How long did he stay in the home?" I told him I did not know because shortly after that, my dad got sick and I had to stop going. I told Clay, "I think about that little precious boy often and wonder how he is doing; I hope and pray his life is much better and he is happy."

A couple of months later, I got a text from Clay, asking if we could meet up that weekend. I responded, "Sure, when?" He texted back, "Saturday morning for breakfast." All week, Clay called or texted to make sure I had planned nothing for that Saturday. I thought it was a little odd, but I said to myself, "Ok." On the

Friday before we got together, Clay called and said, "I have a big day planned! I'm coming to pick you up around 7:00AM." I said, "Wait! What! 7:00AM?!!" He said, "Yep! Be ready!" and started laughing. He said, "Seriously, 7:00AM, no later than 7:30AM." Saturday morning, my doorbell rang and it was Clay, excited and ready to go. We got in the car and Clay said, "Ok, we are going to have breakfast and you are going to volunteer with me at the elementary school." He said, "I have worked everything out and later, you get to meet my mentee." Now, I was thinking to myself, "He really did plan this day." At breakfast, Clay told me that, "kids at the elementary school are going to tease me" and blushingly smiled. "Why are they going to tease you? I asked. "I have brought family and friends to volunteer with me, and they have always been males. I've never brought a female before," Clay responded. I said, "Oh, this is going to be fun!" Then, we both laughed. On our way to the elementary school, Clay said, "I'm bringing them ice cream. They all had such a great week; I like to bring them treats from time to time." We arrived at the school, walked in, and the kids started screaming, "Mr. Clay! Mr. Clay! The next words I heard were, "Who is this, Mr. Clay?" Clay introduced me to the kids. We listened to them, played, and talked with them, watched them show us dance moves, and then danced with them. Then, we brought out ice cream. It was like we told them we were taking them all to Disney World; it felt so good to see those kids so excited and happy. On our way back to the car, I told Clay, "That felt really good, hanging out with your kids." And like a little kid, I said, "Where are we going now?" Clay looked at me and laughed, then said, "We are going to have lunch with my mentee." We pulled up to this quaint restaurant with a patio overlooking a lake and a walking path. We found a table, and Clay told the host we were expecting someone. Clay said, "A couple of months ago, you shared with me about the child that grabbed your heart at your volunteer group. When you said his name was Jax, it got my attention." Clay continued, to say, "You see, my mentee's name is Jaxson Evan. When he was finally adopted, his parents wanted to give him a fresh start so they started to use his middle name, Evan." As I listened to Clay, my heart skipped a beat and he could tell I was feeling some type of way. He saw it in my face. I could not believe what I was hearing! I prayed for the moment that I could see Jax, again; I wanted to know that he was doing well and healthy and my prayer was coming true. WOW!! I could not believe it! As I sat there in awe, our waitress walked up and asked for our drink order. Clay looked at me, turned to the waitress and said, "Right now we will take water." Clay looked at me and said, "Are you ok?" I laughed and said "Yes." I asked Clay, "How long have you been mentoring him?" Clay responded, "Ummmm, it's been five or six years." Clay went on to say how, in the beginning, it was rough. A couple of years before I met him, he was just adjusting to the couple that adopted him. I started to ask another question, and in walked Jaxson Evan. This young man was 6ft tall, medium build, clean cut, and very handsome. Clay and I stood up to greet Jaxson Evan. "Evan, this is…" and before Clay could finish introducing us, Jaxson Evan and I just grabbed and hugged each other. Jaxson Evan said, "I remember you so well!" I said emotionally, "You know I have been praying for you for so many years!" Evan said, "Yes Ma'am, I know. Thank you for praying for me!" Clay said, "WOW!! The smiles on you all's faces… PRICELESS!" When we finally sat down, our waitress came back, took our order, and said, "You guys make a beautiful family!" That is when my tears started falling. Clay said to Evan and I, "Y'all know this is nobody but God bringing us together like this." All of us smiled; my tears were falling even more. Evan reached out to me, grabbed my hand, and said, "It's ok." Clay began to share with me, "After you left the children's home, a couple came in several months later and adopted him." He went on to say, "The couple was not able to have children, but they had a big heart to help people, especially children." Evan proclaimed, "They were and are God's blessing to me! He said, "The first few years of my life with this couple who took a major chance on me, I gave them challenge after challenge." He laughed and said, "I was a little brat and they loved me more and more." Evan said humbly, "They are my angels, just like you were."

After dinner, the three of us went on the walking path and talked. We sat down on a bench, Clay on my left and Evan on my right. Evan shared with me how he used to be so withdrawn and mean. He said, "I wanted my real mom; I did not want a substitute. I was mad because, for whatever reason, she could not be my mom." Evan said, "My adoptive parents found this boys group that was in our neighborhood and enrolled me. That was how I met Clay and things got better." Evan shared, "Clay and his fraternity showed us we had to look at things past what we already knew." He said, "They would tell us, that we had to look deep to find the truth. Once we found the truth, we would have everything we need." I was so proud listening to him, so intelligent and smart. My prayers were certainly answered. Evan said, "I never told Clay this, but I researched my name, Jaxson Evan." Clay looked at him and said, "What?" I'm looking at him, listening intently. "Yes, I looked deep to find out what my name meant, isn't that what you taught me?" Clay sat up and looked at him. Evan said, "With my childhood, I was curious. I figured my name had to mean something." He believed he could have been named anything. He said, "Why Jaxson Evan?" And he was right! Evan had us take our cellphones out to see for ourselves.

Clay and I took out our cellphones, Evan said, "Look up Jaxson. The English meaning is, 'God is gracious and God has shown favor.'" When I looked it up, Evan was right. "Now, look up, Evan," he said. We looked the name Evan up and it said, "God is gracious and the Hebrew meaning is rock." Evan dug deep to find the truth and now, he has everything. He has loving and wonderful parents who taught him to help people; they taught him to be appreciative and respectful. Once Evan got on track, he studied hard to make good grades, and now, he is getting ready to graduate from high school with honors. He has a few full-ride scholarships… he is doing great!! Evan said, "I realized my situation could have been much worse. I also recognize my situation was tough, but I made it through." He said, "To add, the two of you were very instrumental in making sure I was cared for." And he said, "Above everything, I understand that God allows things to happen so that we can know in our hearts who He is, and all that He has done for us. He went on to say, "Had I not gone through what I went through, I would not be who I am now and had the desire to help kids with similar stories." Evan announced, "I am going to earn my degree in Child Psychology and I am designing a program for abused children to go through so they can heal." He looked at us and said, "God is gracious!"

Each day, God shows us that He hears our prayers, especially our concerns we hold close to our hearts. He may not respond right then to our prayer, BUT God does answer. I declare, *in everything, I will give thanks to God, for this is God's will for you in Christ Jesus. 1 Thessalonians 5:18*

L'Tarra Moore is the daughter of Pastor George Moore (deceased) and Mrs. Nettie- Lewis Moore. She taught Basic Computers to 3-4 year olds at Saint Philip Child Development Center for 10 years. She is now working on the Marketing Team at Saint Philip A.M.E. Church. She loves to encourage and help people. She is now enhancing her education by going back to school to study Instructional Design and her new venture in writing.

※ VELMA RAMOS ※

The Hats of Life Lessons

The Hats of Life Lessons

A t the age of five I started to realize my mother had a special gift. She birthed five girls and two boys. Mom also raised a stepdaughter from her husband, and other children she adopted throughout the years. She married young, and after many years of mental and emotional abuse she decided to divorce her husband.

Mother pursued her college degree in social services and worked in a nursing home for many years. She would take early shifts so she could be home in time to take care of us kids because she didn't believe in babysitters or daycares.

I considered my mother my hero, and she worked hard at keeping that title. She always told us to work hard at whatever you do in life and your dreams can be accomplished. She taught her daughters how to not rely on men but be independent, and taught her sons that a good woman should be cherished. My mother demanded respect and didn't have to say things twice. Mom's facial expression alone would be punishment enough, because you knew if she told you twice, you were going to get that whipping! Mother had us trained so well that when the street lights blinked on you knew you'd better be turning the corner on your way home with your bike. The Bible says in *Eph.*

6:1, "children obey your parents so that you may live a long life." This was the Scripture we lived by.

Although my mother had a special gift for raising children, she wore many hats in life. Her first hat was her dedication for her children, as well as other people's children, that she made her own. She was what we called the "neighborhood mom", and would feed all of our friends. My sisters and I became smart and started choosing which friends could come into our home to eat, because everyone wasn't our real friend. Mom bought clothing and shoes for our friends if we told her their mom couldn't afford them. Now, as a child you become selfish, but don't question your mother. But I did ask her once if we were rich because I felt we were. Mom's answer was, "no, we're blessed." I did learn later that mom was teaching us that if you give, God will bless you in return. This also helped me understand why she made us put all our Sunday school money into the offering tray.

Because mom worked in a nursing home she wore the hat of a nurse: She was like our nurse-- when we became ill, mom would bring all our meals and medications to our bedside, and nurture us back to health.

My mom wore the hat of an educator-- she believed in book-smarts and the book of life. She taught her daughters and sons to love and honor God first, respect others, love yourself and respect your body. Mom had a strong passion for families sticking together and our family was like a chain unbroken. She taught us how to plant our feet, but to rely on one another. Although we fought and argued like siblings do, but she always made us apologized. When we came home from school, dinner would be on the table. Mom made sure we ate together so that we could share our day with her. Afterwards we would clear the table for homework and read books. Our teachers never had to worry if we did our homework because once completed we would store it into our book bag.

My mom also wore the hat of a landlord and taught her children how to work on and maintain our apartment building (paint walls, tile floors, put up drywall, do repairs, etc.) When other children had spring break, we had cleanup week and learned how to become landlords.

After many years of bringing children into our home my mother wore the hat of an advocate for adopted children. Mom's God given gift was listening to the heart of the children. She joined the Department of Children And Family Service organization where she served on their board for many years. As we developed into teenagers we continued having other people's children in and out of our home. Some of the children were our friends who stayed one or two nights, while others were children mom started to foster. Mom fostered many children of varies races and also adopted children, which added more sibling to the family. We now had a family of eight girls and two boys.

I learned later in life, my mother was adopted. When asking about her experience as an adopted child it was something she didn't care to share, due to the abuse she experienced from her adopted parents. I began to understand my mother more, not because she loved children, but how God gifted her with a special love.

She experienced some sad moments in her early-adulthood, such as when she lost her second son David at the age of five due to a childhood illness. Mom would tell us about him to keep his memory alive. She then lost another child, my sister Marcia, at the age of seventeen, and later an adult daughter. Although her heart was broken, she knew God had a better plan. I couldn't imagine the pain my mom must have felt losing her children. She always had a way of keeping her children memories alive, by keeping pictures of everyone around the house and large photos albums.

As we all became young women, it was time to have the talk about the birds and the bees. At this point mom wore the hat of a sex-education teacher. Now we were at the dating age, and mom had strict rules around dating. My big brother had to be with us on the date to make sure there was no funny business.

Mother was a God-fearing woman all her children had to stay in Sunday school and church service every week. If you didn't go to church, you weren't allowed outside afterwards. We were the family that prayed together and stayed together-- mother wouldn't have it any other way.

As the years went on many of my older sibling started to pursue their education. One of my sisters went into the military and fought in the war. Another sister and I received our bachelor's degree in social services. My brother decided to accept a computer technician job, and later furthered his education on the job. Another sister married and moved south with her husband, where she managed a restaurant. Some of the children my mother adopted are doing well for themselves and have pursued careers in mortuary science, veterinary assistance, etc.

One day, mother decided to sell the big house where we grew up. Then she stopped renting her other property and moved into it herself, along with other children she fostered until her late seventies.

My mother wore many hats and each one taught us a lesson. Her children would not be the women or men we are today if God had not given us the mother he wanted us to have.

On February 18, 2017 at the age of 83 my mother Mary Anderson left her earthly life to a heavenly life. She's wearing the best hat now, and her legacy has continued to pass on to her grandchildren.

This Mother Of Mine

This mother of mine surprises me each and every time. Wherever she goes she finds the time to look so fine. Sunday morning, she takes out her fineness hat. I watch as she sits to prepare herself for church to praise her God. I look at her and say "Mama, you have the best hats, but why red today?" She softly says "Because of the blood of Jesus", and she must pray for all the children.

This mother of mine has the greatest mind she reaches out to the children and brings them home. She loves them and nurtures their wounds. She follows her heart and mind and the gift that God gave her. God is looking down upon her and sees the good things she does, and when she gets to heaven she will receive her reward.

This mother of mine looks to the heavens and speaks to her God asking for blessing for the children, for they are sinners and know not what they do. She asks the Father to bless her, to feed them when they are hungry, to clothe them when they are cold, and to love them when they feel unloved. She says this prayer "in the name of Your son Jesus Christ."

The Courage To Love

The courage to love ourselves is something we have to work on every day of our lives.

This should be a daily practice.

But as you know there is the world and environment around us.

Forming relationships with our friends and family can influence the way we feel about certain things.

People who are hurting emotionally bring their pain with them everywhere they go.

When we hurt, we hurt others without being aware.

If we never heal the pain and the hurt, it will keep us off balance.

The neglected wounds of our past are the major source of our misery.

Sometimes to understand people is to reach into their life history, to know who they are

Everyone is a make-up of their past, whether it was challenging or non-challenging.

Some of us never leave our past, and this hinders us from moving toward our future and purpose in life.

Our childhood experiences affect our way of life as an adult.

If these experiences were negative, then we have to make changes in our adult lives to love ourselves and move toward the positive things we want to see happen in our lives.

We can't change people.

People have to want to change themselves.

We can offer suggestions, advice without judgment, and love without conditions

Let go and let God.

Velma Ramos is from Chicago Illinois, she received her bachelor degree in Social Service from Northeastern Illinois University. Her passion is helping people of all walks of life. She's worked as a Domestic Violence advocate for over twenty five years. In her spare time Velma enjoys writing poetry. Each year during domestic violence month she showcase her writing skills through a stage play called Women of the Purple Rose. Velma enjoys cooking and spending time with her family.

≫ LORETTA SCOTT ≪

Daffodil's Blues

Daffodil's Blues

Chapter 1

There was nothing eccentric about Daffodil's behavior, many of her neighbors thought. They whispered to each other as her long, lean legs strutted briskly past them down the stairs onto the street toward the Botanical Gardens. This had become a pastime for Daffodil; her way to venture out the same time every Wednesday... it was a promise she had made to herself 17 years ago...and she kept to that promise month after month, week after week, and year after year never missing one Wednesday. Daffodil's commitment would be different she thought this year; a flower will bloom.

Daffodil had a secret, like many young women who are placed in horrific compromise situations with no support systems. She held her secret close, locked away in her heart...a secret that caused her suffering, bound, and sometimes, full of doom, yet she vowed to keep silent or speak on it as long as she had breath.

Still, she would awaken every Wednesday; early in the morning, before the sunrise, scrub her skin fiercely being careful not to bruise it, showered in her favorite cherry-blossom bath gel, put on her very basic but elegant blue linen dress, fancy her hair in an up-do sweep with a final touch of a small rose hair-pin; cute she thought, step into her Nine-West blue-leathered pumps, place a dash of her favorite Passion perfume on each side of her neck, after her transformation she glanced into the mirror, admired herself, and headed straight for the Gardens.

The neighbors who experienced this ritual on their Brownstone's steps every Wednesday waved and made room for her as she stepped carefully down the worn cemented stairs while she held firmly to the iron-cast rail as she excused herself to pass them. A few of their plastic faces giggled in silence as she walked by, while two of them held their hands over their mouths to keep the laugher within. Most of them considered her a strange, eccentric woman, mumbled after she passed, and said how she never had a suitor or any visitors; yet most of them continued to smile at her as if they cared. She was smarter than they knew, and she somehow knew the smiles, waves, and politeness were not at all genuine, but she did not care about their thoughts of her, this was her place, she thought, and she had a right to be.

The garden was her place where she could find solitude, peace, and serenity, and in some crazy way a rebirth of her almost lost inner soul. How her face glowed with joy as she gazed at the flowers of many colors, and how they held close to their roots planted in their soil. The only thing missing was the root of her existence that had become a hole in an area of her heart, which bled silently so many times before, she thought.

Chapter 2

Daffodil kept her promise to keep connected to her roots, so year after year, she visited the Garden, and year after year, she sat on the same stone bench that had become worn with some of its marble stones missing. She reminisced about what could have been; and how her life may have been different if she would have made other choices. But it was easier for her to accept the cloudy days as she went back in time to remember, wishing she could erase those thoughts, that day, that person, and hoping everyday she would forget the pain that held her captive, and tormented. She wished it could all go away; but the beauty of those flowers of daffodils, roses, hyacinths, callies' and daisies kept calling her as if the root she had detached a long time ago was there waiting for her every Wednesday, week after week, month after month, and year after year.

Their blooms were iridescent giving off their aroma as if to say, "I'm alive"; from the smell of sweetness, yet in some small way...Daffodil felt alive when she visited the garden, although she was spiritually asleep, locked and denying herself for years, the removal of men in her life...no one to call her own...the constant isolation, but today her silent screams inside would set herself free, free to forgive herself, free to remove the shackles that led her to the garden week after week, month after month , year after year, while she met with the imaginary root she held close to her heart, a denied root of her own existence that was forced to bloom on its own; "that was denied from the very beginning". She went through years of grief, regret, and depression, and blamed herself for a selfish act she had no control of. Oh, how she hated that she had wasted so much time to reconnect, to forgive, and to find peace. She thought of the many times she wanted to give up, and allowed the enemy to win; the long nights of studying, and crying at the same time because she had no one to talk to. There were so many times she would reach for her cell phone only to put it down because she could not allow someone else in her world.

Chapter 3
Almost like Yesterday, Daffodil speaks…

The monster took hold in my life 17 years before, the wind gushed against the windows while the rain pounded furiously against the screens; the rain was so intense and rough I thought it was going to break the glass. A fierce storm had come through town, and I, being a little Daffodil was alone with my "grandfather." It was one of those nights that I dreaded to sleep alone because I feared the thunder and lightning, or for that matter, wanted to be left alone. I was just a mere simple young teenager, learning to find myself, learning how to explore, still jumping rope with my friends, experiencing who I was. I was also beginning to like and appreciate those thick pigtails that bounced against my back when I jumped double-Dutch rope with my friends, and the small buds on my chest were beginning to take shape as breasts which I tried not to notice; but I was still trying to like my skinny legs. I had recently started my menstruation, and required female protective napkins monthly. I was becoming a young woman, and was petite, my mother would say, my small frame somehow fitted my skinny legs. But this night I would meet the ultimate test that would forever change my life, and become engraved as a sore spot in my heart and mind forever.

My grandfather had been always silly, I thought, his silly jokes that were not funny made many laugh at them anyway. He was always doing something in the closed shed… but sometimes I would see him, watching, and staring at me through the dingy spider webbed window while he sipped on his hidden brandy away from my mother. "I would not have dared tell anyone!" Daffodil thought, it was cool with me…but I am sure Pastor Lily

Wentworth, and the church congregation would have thought otherwise.

Sometimes being alone with him while my mother diligently worked at night as an aide would get scary, especially when he looked at me as if his thoughts were nowhere near thinking like a grandfather, and his touches were a little more than his usual at times. I thought nothing more about it, but each day began to get extreme. But he was my grandfather, and his crazy behavior was probably on the days when he drank too much, I thought. I could have never imagined him thinking anything else, after–all, he was my sweet old grandfather. The house shuddered, and the thunder beam of lightning pierced the opening of the worn-torn open of the blinds, and the lights flickered on and off as if it had a mind of its own. I was scared, more than the last time, as the thunder and lightning spoke different languages of loud, explosive noises, and the rain hit hard against the shutters, as the shutters outside the house banged back and forth against the house; that was the last draw, I thought, I had to find refuge, and made a run to my grandfather's room. I remembered him, saying, "I was waiting to see how long you could stand it", but I never gave that comment any thought then; all I knew I was safe in my grandfather's arms. As he tucked me in his bed, he lay beside me, I could feel his rough big hands on my arms, and he gently strokes my hair, his face lends in towards my face, he appeared so big as if he was a monster, and his breath smelled horribly rank of the hidden stale brew brandy. He and his breath nauseated me when he lightly kissed my cheeks, and then my forehead. I was afraid, and numb, but this time not of the rain and thunder, but my grandfather's behavior. I lay there, and allowed him to have his way with me; I never uttered a word to stop him, and he proceeded, and continued to whisper incoherent, and foul words I cannot remember or dared to in my ear.

My grandfather was a big man about two-hundred and fifty pounds of beefy flesh, and his belly hung slightly over his pants, and protruded against the velveteen robe he had on. He instructed me that everything was going to be alright, and continued to tell me, he was here to take care of me…and suddenly I felt his wet lips pressing against mine. I wanted to regurgitate, but I swallowed my fear in silence. All I could smell was his smelly brew stale brandy breath. Then all of a sudden I felt as if I had fallen, and was taken up into a whirlwind of horrible pain: my innocence was never to be no more. I had been violated, my purity of a little girl was gone… forever, and from then on, I did not feel like a young girl again.

His weight almost smothered me, it was finally over, and the lightning and thunder had also ceased. He told me not to mention what had happened to nobody or else I was going to meet my fate with death…and I did just as he had instructed me to. He ordered me to wash myself, and he kissed me on my cheek. I ran to the bathroom, and fell on my knees feeling the chill from the floor. I cried, and cried; the snot running from my nose. I was feeling so alone, and as I look down to the floor, and I began to scream in horror, and quickly remembered what my grandfather had warned me, and I screamed silently while holding my hand over my mouth as I watched my chest rise fast up and down as if my heart was going to beat out of my chest.

Chapter 4

My grandfather's stern voice echoed in my brain, and his last words----"Don't ya tell nobody, ya hear, this is our secret." As I watched, he struggled to fasten his wrinkled overalls; the blue faded smelly overalls penetrated my nostrils with an aroma of a sour-foul stench, and I still can remember that night. He said he was sorry, but said I had asked for it, "running round the house in those short dresses exposing those soft, young legs, and keeping my legs apart when I sat in a chair; and his wish preys on me, day after day, and every chance he had to receive me, he would have his way with me again, and again-until my stomach began to have a bump, and I began to slowly grow bigger, and bigger, and bigger. I was numb, scared, and angry, but angry with myself because my grandfather said it was my entire fault, and I believed him, and I believed I asked for it for many years. My stomach was growing swollen, and I was becoming sick all the time; I was not able to keep food down and I did not know what to do. When I went to school, I wore tight fitting clothes. There was a time when I borrowed my mother's girdle, and she had no clue.

When my mother saw I was not behaving like I normally did, and was becoming more isolated, she questioned me, and took me to see the doctor reluctantly…I was pregnant, 7 months, and the father of my unborn child was no other than my grandfather. I believed my mother knew, she never questioned me of who it might be, but she refused to support me. She became distant at times, and was ashamed of me. She expressed I had embarrassed the family, and said I was going to be homeschooled, and give the baby up for adoption. A part of me truly did not care anymore, I did not want to have the baby, but a part of me was angry because he was a part of me. The monster did not ease off, and although I was unable to have intimacy with my grandfather, he would force me to do other things to him when my mother was at work. I hated him, but I felt trapped, I had no one to tell.

Chapter 5

My son was born in the season of a cold winter day. As soon as he was delivered, I was not able to see him, but in my heart, I did not want to; I hated him, just as I have hated my grandfather for all those months, and years of abuse. My son was given to local parents who shortly moved to New York. I knew they would love, and care for him, and he was a memory in my life I wanted to forget.

I was homeschooled until high school, I received my High School diploma, but my heart was eager to get away, to start anew, and to forget the old South I have come to despise. Nothing had changed-- my grandfather was getting feeble, and for some reason he did not force me to do those nasty things anymore, but he kept a close watch on me, and every now and then he would touch on me but he never entered me again. I think it was because I became pregnant, and he was scared. Despite my silence, I never told anybody other than God. Sometimes I was angry with God because he allowed it to happen, but I always heard a voice saying, "a lesson to learn and a soul to reach".

I applied for colleges farther away, and was accepted into the New York University School of Law. I anxiously, and secretly packed my clothes in a wooden suitcase that one time belonged to my grandmother. I saved my money and bought a one-way ticket, and boarded a Greyhound bus.

Chapter 6

Years Later

Once she arrived in New York, she stayed at a rooming house, got hired at a Department store, and on the weekends worked as a waitress. It was hard, she remembered, but the tips were good. She enrolled in college, and life began to look up for her, as she worked day and night. Daffodil was busy working and studying, and rarely had time for church.

During the years, she saw several psychiatrists, took various medications for depression from Zoloft to Prozac, but nothing ever seemed to combat her despair, her loneliness, and the guilt she had. She decided to call home, and learned her aging grandfather had died of a sudden heart attack. She was furious about the heart attack-- she thought "that's all? God should have allowed a harsher painful death or some other severe punishment than him dying of an old man heart attack!" She was relieved he was dead, but had lived in a prison herself for some years, and did not attend the funeral.

She graduated from law school, passed the bar exam, felt excited, yet also felt something was missing in her life. She later worked for a family practice law firm. For many years she was bitter and cold. One day while she was reviewing a case, she began to have this urgency to see her son, and wanted to know what he had become. She called her estranged mother, but her mother refused to tell her where he was, or who had adopted him. She began to search for him herself, and later hired a private investigator to look for him. The private investigator located him, and informed her that her son was living in Brooklyn, New York, a long way from Mississippi, where she had given birth to him, and had vowed never to visit again. She called him, and asked him to meet with her; he did not know who she was or what she had wanted. She thought, "He was so vulnerable, and easy to manipulate like his mother, but maybe he knew who she was, and was waiting for this day." She asked him to meet with her on Wednesday at the Botanical Gardens in Brooklyn, and he said he would. Strange as it may sound, he never hesitated as if he already knew who she was.

Chapter 7

She arrived early that day to avoid him seeing her enter. A few minutes had passed, and more minutes, and she was beginning to think he wasn't going to show…but just when she began to feel jilted "like a stood-up date", a handsome young man walked through the entrance. He was tall, almost 6 feet tall, quite tall for his age, she thought as she imagined his estimated age to be right, his pecan complexion was almost like hers, and his skin appeared smooth, his hair was cut close to his head, and his clothing was neat. He wore blue, khaki pants, and a light blue shirt with a brown belt that showed he was well coordinated and well fitted to go with his lean statue that resembled hers. She thought how happy she was, and for the first time her eyes saw her son…She wanted to call his name aloud; feel his skin against hers; she wanted to rub his head and lightly kiss his cheeks; she wanted to touch him, but she did not want to open any more old wounds. Daffodil encouraged her mind to lose concentration, and to refocus on why she came there. She looked at the flowers, and lost her train of thoughts of the "what if", and concentrated on the many colors as if she was in a trance. Daffodil thought for the first time, she had finally seen her lost root, and in some way she felt like her life could be complete, and her curiosity was resolved. Daffodil held her head down in disbelief, and a tear began to roll down her face, it was not tears of pain, but she was relieved she came to fill the void she needed so long to do, and in a strange way to set herself free. She looked up and on the other side, she saw her son, a handsome young man sitting poised, gazing at the beautiful flowers, waiting. Unfortunately, she got cold feet, and could not bring herself to greet him; she had preferred to leave the past in the past. Daffodil inhaled deeply, exhaled, smiled, and wiped the tear from eyes, and walked towards the exit door... she look back at her son to see if he had seen her, but he was preoccupied with the beauty of the flowers as she had been for so many years. She then shook her head lightly as if to say "it is done," smiled, and while she strolled quietly out the gold-frame-glass doors, she whispered underneath her breath, "Thank God, I'm free, no more Daffodil's Blues!" She left never to look back, but to look forward to the happiness she deserved.

Forward

Incest is never an option, or is it ever the victim's fault. Daffodil was a victim of someone she trusted and loved, as with many people who are sexually abused. Today there are many resources available that can assist a victim if they have been violated. Don't allow abuse to win. For Daffodil she was able to rise above her wounded heart, and scars and break through to become an advocate for abused victims, and committed lawyer practicing family law. Silence is never an option...Scream.

 Loretta Scott is a published author of "Yes I Can, an Army Nurse story before, during, and after Desert Storm. She is retired from the military as an Army Nurse. She resides in the state of Maryland. She remains active as a nurse, and believer of Christ. She

has three beautiful children who reside in other states, with one son retired from the Army. She is a proud grandmother of five grandsons. Currently, she is working on several books soon to be published. God's Speed.

❋ NORMIA VÁZQUEZ SCALES ❋

The Portal: Rendering, A Sparked Epiphany

The Portal: Rendering, A Sparked Epiphany

C hronic fatigue, and drenched monsoonal fever plagued me
as I arose that subarctic December day. It was just shy
of two years ago, and labored as an utmost disheartening
cornerstone of my fortified memory. Nevertheless, I oozed out
of my majestic quarters and into an abruptly invigorating shower,
prior to transporting my beloved son, Máximo off to primary
academia.

Upon crossing the threshold of my modest employer, I'd
been graced by lush and flamboyant poinsettias. Moreover,
the tantalizing aroma of gingerbread, coupled with enchanting
Christmas hymns, permeated the luminous corridor. Boisterous
chatter and guttural laughter emanated betwixt and between
colleagues exchanging holiday gifts. Yet, I'd soon discovered that
my division of the establishment had been excluded from the
holiday festivities, despite our figurative blood, sweat and tears.
Namely mine, in exchange for my painstaking contributions. My
pulse hastened, now proportionate to the discomfort in my upper
extremities and I gasped for air amidst my struggle against stress-
induced respiratory affliction.

The overwhelming aura of "void appreciation" consumed me. Meanwhile, I unexpectedly received the disenchanting headline that Máximo had been habitually tormented between school and his evening destination. Hence, the bough had broken... and the cake had become instantly frosted, per se. Needless to say, I'd harnessed the audacity to nosedive into my active "carpe diem" persona and bade my employer farewell. My unprecedented "healthy" leap of faith had suddenly been activated. Therefore, my first heaping dose of selflessness in this budding new chapter had now been scripted.

I vividly recall my unwavering belief that I would attract the ultimate opportunity which encompassed flexibility and prosperity. Therefore, this platinum endeavor would afford me the priceless option of single-handedly retrieving my son from school while yielding ample revenue. The abominable thought of further subjecting my son to "after school bullying," alongside serving a complacent and unappreciative employer, served as the catalyst for acquiring my customized undertaking within a mere thirty-day span. Then, lo and behold, by the "grace of God," my abundant aspiration had been achieved.

In hindsight, I acknowledge that vast and varied members of my circle had deemed me "disillusioned." However, my sound intentions congruent to my vibrant vision and devotion to my Higher Power, enabled a sweet and savory manifestation. In laymen's terms, I'd made the decision.... To jump... in light of the purest rationale, my son... and myself... in that precise order. I segued from one contract assignment to another, successfully completing each project, swinging from project vine to project vine like a female Tarzan.

In the midst of my plethora of feats, I'd landed into an exclusive women's challenge, spearheaded by my esteemed friend and

The Portal: Rendering, A Sparked Epiphany

Spiritual Sister, Bridget Burns-Diarrassouba! What commenced as a fitness challenge had morphed into a humanitarian one. In summary, Bridget implored the members to sow seeds and deeds over an agreed interval. Given the season, I'd opted to challenge myself to rendering "A Deed a Day until Mother's Day" and literally branded it as such. Although opportunity and capital had abundantly surfaced, I hadn't struck oil. However, I committed to another decision...to plunge yet again, sowing a variety of tangible and intangible deeds and seeds, including: "Wounded Warrior Project donations"; Harris Teeter Hero surveys; a post-office food drive and aiding fellow single mothers, to name a few. However, the sheer gratification yielded from each non-begrudging humanitarian effort was second to none.

Unbeknownst to me, I'd opened a portal to an ocean of unanticipated rewards and growth. My entire life and lifestyle had graduated overnight. This stemmed from replacing a dated domestic jalopy with a pristine import and beyond. The overall portrait had been unveiled, confirming the notion that all of my earnest energy, lionhearted efforts and unfaltering gratitude dipped in benevolence had not been in vain. Therefore, a newfound epiphany had been birthed into fruition: One of the keys to the universe is found via "rendering" engulfed in gratitude. "Aha!" This is the rationale behind the cascading waterfall of blessings and redemption flowing into my life since that turning point. This has continued in excess of two consecutive years. Hence, my personalized formula and/or recipe for abundant blessings and fulfillment is as follows:

Abundant Blessings and Fulfillment =
Rendering X Sound Intention X Incessant
Gratitude X Benevolence X Infinity

Yet upon expending infinite time and resources, I've deduced that it's critical to grant myself permission to recharge and regroup in lieu of endless authentic giving. Thus habitual: recalibration, reconfiguration and celebration rests at my disposal.... Indeed at my very fingertips... Bearing the guise of well-warranted, modest and opulent treasures, in which I silently indulged... then... and especially now. Redemption magnified!

Martyrdom

I succumb, utilizing my own positive and
negative "voltage" as a vehicle for jump-starting the
consciousness, drive and ambition of stalled minds
and lost souls...
shedding knowledge, guidance and wisdom while
knowingly compromising.......... my livelihood.

I yield my........ right-of-way, not solely to
uncouth and uncanny motorists and pedestrians, but to
my Supreme Being, the Heavenly Father, prior to
resting head on pillow.

I render my last "100 cents" initially designated for
the Florida tollway... to the maimed Vietnam
Veteran, nearly thrust to his demise, by virtue of
sparing the USA of its sins decades ago.
This demi-Christ motioned to spit-shine my
windshield... yet I declined and resorted
to "Useless 1" aka Biscayne Blvd as an alternate
thoroughfare to my final destination...
I basked in self-contentment throughout this
expedition.

The Portal: Rendering, A Sparked Epiphany

*I relinquished my last morsel of nourishment to the
famished, bastard child in my path, ignoring the
fiery cast iron pangs of hunger mutilating me like
blunt edged spears... yet I prevailed.*

*I paint and plaster my "John Hancock" across stuttered
lines of obscure financial statements in efforts of
scratching a crescent moon smile upon my mother's
pained face... having digested that my script has
just paved the right of passage towards indebtedness
to an Uncle named Sam, whose acquaintance I've never
met.*

*I walked briskly through crossfires, shielding the
newborn fruit of my loins and delivered him as a
dowry to my barren sister.*

*I lend... I bend... I render, then I...........
Buckle-at-the-knee-and-suddenly-collapse...
falling prey to momentary deprivation of my own
consciousness. Yet, merely seconds prior to seizing my
own final breath, I'm resuscitated via the scorching
cup of herbal vitality which prompts me to expel the
fatigue and sheer exhaustion that earlier consumed me.*

*I've been abruptly aroused...
Now, in an intoxicated stupor, I succumb to the
stable hands of this unconventional Physician,
enabling Him to "acupuncture" my supple skin...
welding together my severed mind, body and spirit...
revitalizing me... "metamorphasizing" me... through*

*each strategically positioned needle, bearing the
guise of the breath of life inflating my lungs. He
harmonized my yin and my yang, coupled with the
disproportionate Winter and Summer, rather, Inferno
and Ice churning within me........ after which He*
casts me back onto the battlefield of altars on which
I voluntarily lie from day to day.

*You know I wholeheartedly strive to seal my eyes and
turn my cheek, yet some inexplicable force of nature
sweeps me back to the mercy of those that require...
that crave... that need... that long.. and why? For
having been born onto this planet with
a conscience... my gift and my curse.
I've acknowledged my blatant reality and divine
purpose... That I've been inducted into servitude...
and selfless servants have indeed become a rarity
today... shadowed by the ill demon of greed... yet I
persevere in spite of it all.*

*And you... Have you ingested the meaning of
rendering? To lend, bend and sacrifice going above
and beyond the utmost fragile limbs? Have you
showcased the battle scars spawned from selflessness?
Have you met the casualties entailed in the midst of
true giving and marched down the beaten path of such
unconditionally? If so, please do carry on.
Regardless of the literal and figurative energy it
demands of you... in spite of heartache, betrayal and
discontentment, because only then will merit become
fully unleashed.
Dedicated to President Barack Obama*

Sal-Celian Summer: Fruition Alas

The purposefully abrupt and intrusive clamor ripped her from her graceful slumber upon which she pried and peeled herself from her imperial quarters.

Hence, she indulged in an abbreviated Calgon session by virtue of a searing shower doused in a Caribbean Blue hymn. After momentarily slithering into fitness fare, she summoned her gentleman in waiting, loaded her pristine German import and sliced through the night.

Crowds scampered, sauntered and scurried beneath loudspeakers spewing diplomatic commands... Until the aircraft's residual roaring thunder crushed the sound barrier, signifying the commencement of summer...

Fatigue dissipated... and sheer energy prevailed along the expedition towards the earthy, eclectic, yet chic foundation none other than her grandeur abode... her sanctuary nevertheless. Simple treasures took precedence, encompassing leisurely strolls amid tranquil paved trails... adorned and accentuated with meticulously manicured fields sprinkled with timid does nurturing mannerable fawns and bashful bunnies. Delectable birdsong diffused the atmosphere prior to encroaching dusk. Which beckoned her defiant plunge into the saline pool's depth.

Her ascension above the fluid surface has been graced by iridescent moonbeams in which she basks and marvels... sparking a telepathic conversation... Prior to a tantalizing lunar bath, marking the cessation of the evening and prelude to magnified redemption.

Normia Vázquez Scales

Normia Vázquez Scales (Mia) is a savvy mother, entrepreneur, educator, writer and motivational speaker. Mia passionately advocates and promotes balance to both adults and youth alike via educational mediums such as the nationally renowned AVID Program. However, her comprehensive experience entails Reading/Language Arts Instruction for Miami-Dade Public Schools, coupled with efforts in primary school districts encompassing Illinois and North Carolina, respectively.

Furthermore, Mia's Communications credentialing yielded/birthed from DePaul University has afforded her the opportunity to serve both DePaul and Florida State Universities. Dyson Inc. also labors as a prior landmark which enabled her to engage in International Sales, Marketing and Communications. However, her specialty/niche embodies aiding disadvantaged women and youth yearning to rehydrate, reinvent and become reacquainted with their former and reinvented selves. Mia's spare time is divided between travelling, humanitarian endeavors such as her pro bono "Recalibrating the Scales" teleconference calls, and youth advocacy in primary academia.

Still Available at 81

Still Available at 81

The (A)bsolute (G)reatest (E)vent this side of heaven is here! The "final curtain"; the "last hurrah"; "the end results"; the "worth it all???" time. The "Non-repeat" that has all of its prior events and memories available and subtly interwoven into my "now." I am using it all, to either be optimistic or pessimistic. For me, pessimism is not an option, because my longevity, alone, disallows it! Balance has finally come and I valued myself enough to work in concert with God, Jesus, and the Holy Spirit to arrive at this promised destination-- The place where there is the "peace that passeth all understanding." This unexplainable state is still possible in the midst of a chaotic and unpredictable world. While I expected this phenomenon to change, it didn't, and I was finally able to accept that it was set "AS IS". The only option I had was to re-evaluate and change my perspective of my prior life events in order to arrive at this peaceful state. I fought and fought trying to control the uncontrollable. I made many decisions based on my irrational thinking that the atoms, molecules, protons and matter could be adjusted by me. My struggle has ceased, and now I can laugh at how ridiculous my efforts were. The patience, longsuffering, kindness, and meekness of the "Maker" prevailed. A smile that further illuminates the heavens is on HIS face seeing me open up to a whole new and wonderful experience with HIM, prior to my exit here and entrance there. This little taste of heaven is too much for me, and my tear ducts are working overtime. This is "3D" at its optimum! Everything is magnified in color, importance, and acceptance. I look at an ant, a fly, a fish and a plant as "Creator Choices that make me important because I am a significant and necessary part of their equation. They fit for me and I fit for them. Each moment, hour, and day is anticipated with joyful expectancy. I'm past anxiety, which strongly inhibited this delightful time. I now bulge with excitement bubbles as I walk through taking a breath, walking a step, blinkin" an eye and swallowing! These are the things that matter at this splendid age and were missed due to the unnecessary clutter that enveloped my early life. It seems to be a state of slow motion, intentionally provided by GOD, to allow me to "see". The most disappointing part of aging is that it is ending!! I don't wanna go!!!-- especially now that I have the formula for quality living under my belt that will enable a most appreciative experience and not one of just existing. I wish I had known in previous years what I now know. Life would have maybe been a lot different. The mega bonus came in this season of my life. An answer I had been seeking all of my life. Why did I do what I did and what were my motives? The fantabulous Holy Spirit spent time explaining that ALLLLLLLLLL of my life, I had done and said things to impress people to get their approval and validation. That's a set up for an unending roller coaster ride!!! I needed it though, because I felt unworthy, and although GOD— The Father, JESUS the Son, and the HOLY SPIRIT were always with me, I failed to seek validation from them. They are the only ones who can give it, and I sought it in others. Up and down, up and down, round and around and around and down!! When I accepted the truth, balance started! Transforming still is active--changing anger into adoration, vindictiveness into victory, and worthlessness into worthiness. It ain't ovah..til it's ovah!! God and I had a conversation and I requested check-in time with HIM at age 103!! Guess what, when I renewed my driving plates at age 76, the last three numbers are....yeah, 103. I'm on cruise to be used, I'm available!

MOMMA L's LIFE-LINES

" Serving is satisfying and giving is gratifying "

"The ONLY safe place is in the arms of JESUS "

"Repeat after GOD, The only way is GOD'S way and the way is the WORD

"GOD gives "fact feeling", NOT "flesh feeling" You get HIS facts from HIS WORD and you get satan's facts and feelings from your unclean heart and flesh"... YOUR...CHOICE !!"

"Are you just reading HIS word or are you believing HIS word? There is a difference"

"You can't fight Satan with flesh, he's a spirit! Only SPIRIT can fight spirit! DUH!!"

"Stop acting like victims when you are MORE than conquerors"

"Why are we still asking GOD to do things that HE has given us the authority to do?"

"Love is your intentional gift to others with NO....NO....NO... expectations for anything in return!» Without this, your love credentials are cancelled and those watching will walk away from you , not toward you"

"Prerequisite for assassination: Make a MAJOR minus in the money!"

"Being just with me, there is still an assurance that I am never... no never...alone"

"Me, left with me is a blind spot"

" I'm soooooooooooooooooooooooooo happy!"

"White privilege" omits and excludes me!! Sorry, forgot that I was NEVER included"

"Now that my insides are de-cluttered, my "junk" drawer is now neat!"
"If I weren't a Christian and if I didn't know that this earth realm is wicked, I'd believe that I was a 'pawn' in a chess game"

"I want life to be easy!! It is, if I accept it "AS..IS"

"We stay in trouble because we "stay" in trouble"

"The best things in life AIN'T free! The cost was the CROSS!"

"I wonder what it would be like to experience "di-oppression?"

"I am in such a good place that I love me enough to finally be able to honestly examine my ways"

"Purpose is promise... Pray or Pay"

"Brain food: BIBLE"

"Eat right, enjoy life"

"Listen to quiet, it will speak to you"

"Your constant move in the game of life is obedience"

"Wanna know? GO... SLOW

"Singles: Don't get obsessed with finding a human relationship 'til you have an intimate relationship with the One who makes humans"

"Why are we surprised that this is a sinful world? Why do you think that we were told not to conform to it?"

"GOD not only "IS" but able"

"Let's quit taxing our limited minds trying to figure something out!! HE purposely didn't give us but a little to work with"

"Take the "De" and the "I" out of depression and OBEY what's left!"

Lajuana Weathers is first a servant of God who has been privileged to serve as a "Holistic Vocal Technique Clinician". This has allowed her over the last fifty seven years the opportunity to work with such groups as Chicago Mass Choir, Wooten Choral Ensemble ,Doris Ward Workshop Choral, Mark Hubbard, Rev, Deandre Patterson, Rev. Maceo Woods, Walter Hawkins Music Workshop, Ecclesiates

Community Choir, GMAC, Malcom Williams and Great Faith, Walt Whitman and the Soul Children, and Salem Baptist Church Music Department, and was vocal coach for Pastor Dan Willis of Lighthouse Church with his final singing project" A Man and his Music" and **was honored by** being asked to serve along with Benny Hinn and Lanny Wolfe in Lighthouse's Conference 2016 She retired as Domestic Violence Facilitator with The Center for Domestic Peace and as case manager with the City of Chicago Department of Human Services. Her passion is "giving back" her life experiences on Facebook.

≫ FAY WRIGHT ≪

And Let The Redeemed of The Lord Say So

And Let The Redeemed of The Lord Say So

God is my light in the darkest hour. It is easy to tell a person to hold on and not give up. Yet we do not know the desperation a person is feeling, nor how long they've been feeling that due to issues of molestation, abuse, abandonment, which was my story. We need to be aware of what is making our light dark. How do we hold on when we feel that there is nothing to hold on to, or when all hope is gone and we feel all alone?

WOW!

I lived in darkness twenty plus years until I had a recurring vivid dream, which led to another. I had been molested as a child, a victim of physical and verbal abuse. These dark spirits locked me up subconsciously for years. Due to the intense pain and misery for so long, I tried to commit suicide. Drinking and drugging became my norm to numb my pain, which unknown to me was a plan of the evil one to belong complete destruction to my life and kill me. Who truly knew the desperation of Fay? However, we do have a God that brings us through! Our Father, Who is in heaven, brought me out time and time again from death's door.

I found street activity at the age of 15, which made me drop out of school and move in with my boyfriend. He never physically abused me, but the emotional and verbal abuse was great. He lit cigarettes while coming so close to my skin I could smell the odor of burnt hair on my arms, always reminding me that he would kill me if I cheated on him or left him. My days consisted of smoking weed, reading, and eating ice cream and Doritos. I had to put on presentable outfits, makeup, and do my hair to perfection before he came home from work. The relationship deteriorated further. I wanted to walk seven blocks home to safety, but I was emotionally held captive in that bedroom, held in bondage to the terror in my mind. One Saturday morning after a harrowing night, I put my clothes on, told him I was leaving, walked to the bedroom door, he called my name, I turned, and by a hair-breath, the bullet missed lodging into my head. I took my clothes off, got back into bed, and returned to my sexual duties as if nothing had transpired. Seven months later, Luke 22:43 manifested itself in my life --*"And there appeared an angel strengthening."* I walked out of the relationship terrified, but walked indeed.

My life continued to be completely out of control-drinking, taking drugs, and sexing the elite. The root spirit of molestation was in control. No one ever told me these things were wrong. Never! I did not see it while living that lifestyle.

OH, BUT THE WONDER OF JEHOVAH SAYS ENOUIGH IS ENOUGH! HE MAKES NO MISTAKE! GOD ALMIGHTY ALL BY HIMSELF WILL BRING YOU OUT!

Jesus walked this earth for a reason and you are never alone! Naham 1:7 tell us, *"The Lord is good and a strong pole in a day of trouble; and He knoweth them who trust in Him."* You do have a refuge, a resting place when the world crowds in on you. Run to it!

Stay in it until you are spiritually built up in the marvelous light. (Jude 20) An author and wonderful friend asked me, "What is so powerful that it keeps you in the negative and unable to sustain the positive because of fear?" For me it was a combination of dark spiritual roots, embedded into my fabric of day to day living-- it is natural for Fay; the same as breathing in and out. If I can't breathe, I get the feeling of suffocating. I panic and fight to breathe. This is the same as trying to unshackle anyone from the emotions embedded in their heart. Hopelessness, guilt, shame, being shamed, exhaustion from trying to rise above it. Loneliness, unworthiness, unwillingness, lack of love-- this is what I have known and lived with as constant faithful companions. They were my lifeline, anchoring me down, holding me captive until the mask was ripped off, and again came the fight to breathe. I feel exposed, paralysis sets in, and refuse to take a baby step. What I keep secret germinates and grows; it becomes this giant in my life until it invades every area. And I am rendered powerless to do anything about my circumstances. My thinking is severely warped, I have once again lost all hope. I no longer even try. It costs too much to psyche myself up, and I cover it back up, no matter how miserable I am. I'd rather stay in the norm of misery, where at least I know what to expect and what to do with it. My faithful companions will not let me be tossed to and fro. I can breathe again. Did you notice earlier I said they were my lifeline and not my lifeline? Once the mask was off, I am at times very aware of darkness and despair but now I have a choice because I have been picked up from the hell-hole that I was living in. Yes, I do know Jesus but it does not carry its full power of the blood until I come into the supernatural realm of revelation that He loves me--then and only then can I walk in the footprints of our Savior, convicted of my worthiness to God and self.

Cast all your cares on Him. Have mercy on me, O Lord; please take these Luciferian lies from me! Oh, that You would bless me indeed Abba Father! Just like me, you too will make it through the darkest hour because God has had His Hand on you and still does. Let go of the misery. How? Unseen faith. Cast thy burden upon the Lord, and He shall sustain thee: He shall never suffer the righteous to be moved. Faith without works is dead! Psalms 32:8 promises, "I will instruct thee and teach thee in the way thou shalt go; I will guide thee with mine eye." I am telling you God is powerful! Jesus sees and feels everything you are going through. Don't forget what the enemy comes to do. We do not serve a God of weakness, fear, nor anxiety, cast all your thoughts on Him. He has already told you with His living breathing word that you have been set free. And now it becomes a choice of what you and I am choosing to believe, how do we want to live? Hold on to your seat belt! These next few words will seem abrasive, some may even get slightly offended, and it is okay because you purchased this book for hope. And in everything you want to give praise. Some of us have already arrived, some of us are trying to arrive and some of us who have arrived still struggle. STOP THE DIVISION! STEP UP TO THE PLATE! Do you want our Father who art in heaven to help you? Stop dividing the forces! It is either yes or no!

The power no longer exists in the negative. Lord I know some of me and confess it to you, please release me from judgmental thoughts and words. I do not want any traces of Satan's dirt abiding in me. Father please release from me a gossiping tongue. And I need to be effective. I need God's wisdom, knowledge, perseverance, strength, and with all of this to get and apply understanding to avoid the pitfall of the one who comes to kill, still, and destroy. Any fact facing us is not as important as our attitude toward it! My life today consists of praising God, praying, lifting holy hands to heaven, helping the church, learning what I can about our heavenly Father, loving faith, family, friends, and the brethren. My life is not always in total alignment with God's will, but I attempt to stay prayed up to get me back in line. Standing on the promises of God is not always an easy order to fill, but putting on the whole armor of God has allowed me to learn how to love Fay and stand firm in my position on the battlefield. I have been hit by the fiery darts of the enemy and all I can do is take my armor back to my Creator and have it repaired over and over, expecting beyond anything that I could ever imagine, as I see the manna falling from heaven every day. The blood never loses its power to do exactly what it says it will do. This morning I heard Joel Osteen say *"trouble is inevitable but misery is optional."* But this is what I say-- if you die today, what will people say about you? I heard this at a funeral and it changed my life. It has been an ongoing process and will be until I pass away. God has been telling me for the past five months that HE wants my whole heart. He wants to mend the brokenness and fill it with a love so pure and true for the divine appointments with Him and to impact others. I am willing, and learning to let go of flesh and let Him guide. It is by no means an easy task. I had to learn early to be in control while being in abusive relationships. Oh, believe me when I say that I became a terror to men. I became the one that they used to be. I am thankful for the prayer warriors in my family. It said that the Holy Spirit will not force himself on us, but He has a way through intercession to do what is asked in supplication, and He will infuse our spirit with His Spirit until awareness enters our conscious mind.

Fay Wright

POEM

My sister passed away on Mother's day 2016. I was her main caretaker for over a month. Even though my heart has shattered into a million painful pieces, still God is worthy of praise. Even though my tears fall so heavily, yet still God is worthy to be praised.

Finally my redeemer is satisfied with me, yes; He is so worthy to be praised, as I put my hand in my Father's hand. Now the question is this for my loved ones: Is God satisfied with the way you have chosen to live? Will God be able to say "welcome home my true and faithful servant? Fix it with your Savior while there is still time.

Find him before it is too late. With heartfelt prayer from Fay and Margaret. Matthew 17:7, 8 --"*And Jesus came and touched them and said arise, and be not afraid. And when they lifted up their eyes, they saw no man, save Jesus only.*"

My name is Fay Wright and I reside in Lynchburg, Virginia where I was born and raised. I am the proud mother of three beautiful daughters, Brandy, Kamika, and Kelly, along with my twelve wonderful grandchildren. I have the privilege of enjoying my mother as she is still in the land of the living. My aunts are my lifeline that have been a great inspiration to me during my challenging struggles. My desire is to equip myself for the call as a Minister of the Lord Jesus Christ by attending Liberty University seminary this fall. For those who desire to read my book in its entirety or be ministered to, I can be reached at wrightfay15@gmail.com

(SPECIAL THANK YOU TO REGINA BARBOUR,7DOGSRUNNING EXTRA THANK YOU TO BISHOP T.D. JAKES AND DR.BILL WINSTON FOR BEING MY SPIRITUAL EAR AND EYEGATES FULL OF WISDOM AND KNOWLEDGE!)

Made in the USA
Middletown, DE
22 July 2017